M000247391

The Inns & Outs of Collecting

How Bed & Breakfast Owners Use Collections to Decorate

Sherry White

Published by  Hobby House Press
Grantsville, Maryland 21536
www.hobbyhouse.com

Every effort has been made to insure that the information presented is accurate. Since we have no control over physical conditions, individual skills, or chosen tools and products, the publisher nor the author assume no liability or responsibility for any loss arising from the use of this book.

Additional copies of this book may be purchased at $22.95 (plus postage and handling) from
Hobby House Press, Inc.
1 Corporate Drive, Grantsville, MD 21536
1-800-554-1447
www.hobbyhouse.com
or from your favorite bookstore or dealer.
©2002 Sherry White

All rights reserved. No part of this book may be reproduced or utilized in any form or by any means, electronic or mechanical, including photocopying, recording, or by an information storage and retrieval system, without permission in writing from the publisher. Inquiries should be addressed to Hobby House Press, Inc. 1 Corporate Drive, Grantsville, MD 21536.

Printed in the United States of America

ISBN: 0-87588-643-4

Acknowledgments

There are many people that I would like to thank for assisting me in publishing this book. First, I would like to thank each of the bed and breakfast owners who took time out of their busy schedules to provide me with the information I needed. Without them, this book literally could not have been. Also, I'd like to thank the team at Hobby House Press who encouraged me to create this book, especially Brenda Wiseman and Theresa Black. Thanks to Gary Ruddell for giving me the opportunity to test the waters. Finally, I'd like to thank my family — my husband, Aaron, and my mother, Loretta, for their encouragement and for taking care of Gabriella and Ian at nights and on weekends when I needed to "work on my book."

Dedication

To my daughter, Gabriella Faith, and to my son, Ian Paul.
It's the time of your life, so live it well.

To my best friend, Aaron.

To Mom.

Table of Contents

Introduction 7
Rules for Collecting 8
Pointers for Displaying Collectibles 10

Home Furnishings 13

The Queen Victoria® — Arts and Crafts Furniture 14

The Arbor Rose — Boxes 16

55 East —Art 18

Augusta House — Eastlake Furniture 20

Housewares 23

Waterloo Country Inn — Coffee Grinders 24

Inn at Norwood — Teapots/Teacups 26

Inn at Stockbridge — Pewter 28

Bittersweet Farm — Crocks and Pantry Boxes 30

The Parsonage on the Green — Teapots/Teacups 32

The Villa — Napkin Rings 34

Acacia House — Saucers/Plates 36

Fitch Hill Inn — Railroad Dinnerware 38

Lynn's Inn — Rare Books 40

Pottery and Glass 43

The Golden Pheasant — Quimper Pottery 44

The Deerhill Inn — Yellow Ware Pottery 46

Desert Dove — Watt Pottery 48

The Notchland Inn — Cobalt Glassware 50

Wedgwood Inn — Wedgwood China 52

Stone Soup Inn — Hand-painted China 54

The Brickhouse Inn — Pharmacy Bottles 56

Gracehill — Purses 84

Gwendolyn's Inn — Vintage Clothing 86

Great Valley House of Valley Forge —
   Vintage Wedding Dresses 88

Colonel Taylor — Quilts 90

Los Poblanos Inn — Samplers/Beadwork 92

Decorative 95

Pinnacle Vista Lodge — Snowbabies 96

Candlewyck Inn — Baskets 98

Wolcott House — Smoking Paraphernalia 100

Whistling Swan Inn — Longaberger Baskets 102

Alexander Hamilton House — Shadow Boxes 104

Pleasant Springs Farm — Sheep 106

Directory 108

Charley Montana — Fire King Dishes 58

B&B at Taylor's Corner — Danish Porcelain 60

Whispering Pines — Pottery 62

Toys 65

Cameo Rose Victorian Country Inn — Dolls 66

Country Life — Teddy Bears 68

The Dolls' House — Dolls 70

Rosewood Country Inn — Teddy Bears 72

Chez Amis — Teddy Bears 74

Mill Creek Homestead — Dolls 76

Textiles 79

The Red Barn Bed & Breakfast — Quilts 80

The Old Brick Inn — Vintage Tablecloths 82

Introduction

My first experience at a bed and breakfast was as a newlywed. My husband and I and several of our guests traveled from New Jersey to my hometown in Maryland for the ceremony. The small town had very few resources as far as accommodations went, so nearly all our family and guests from New Jersey stayed at the one nearby hotel. Not wanting to spend our honeymoon with relatives and friends, we were able to locate a bed and breakfast in the area. It was perfectly charming. The 19th century brick home was reminiscent of the Civil War era and smelled of many years of cozy wood fires blazing in the fireplace. We enjoyed a wonderful breakfast with other guests who congratulated us — not at all the experience we would have had at an impersonal hotel. As we left, the morning fog was just beginning to lift from the surrounding fields. What a wonderful way to begin our grand adventure as a married couple.

A few years later, we decided to go to Colonial Williamsburg, and anyone who has visited the historical area knows just how many magnificent bed and breakfast inns there are to choose from. We stayed in a cozy inn within walking distance to the historical district. Again, our experience left us with wonderful memories. From then on, we decided that when we went out of town, we would do everything we could to stay at an inn. The hominess and good company of a bed and breakfast didn't compare with the sterile and impersonal hotel environment.

Our interest in history and our love of old homes led us back to Historic Williamsburg a few years later during the Christmas holidays where we stayed at another inn even closer to the historic district. At that time, we were beginning to think about buying our own home so we started looking at the details of the bed and breakfasts in which we were staying. We had always loved the houses and decorations, but now we took special note of what we liked and what we would change to incorporate into our own home. That's exactly what I hope you, the reader, will do after reading this book. My intention is to show you how creative innkeepers have chosen to use their collections to decorate their awe-inspiring inns so that you may take special note of what you like and what you would do differently in your own home.

Rules for Collecting

As the saying goes, one man's junk is another man's treasure. I have a great-uncle who lived through the depression so he doesn't believe in waste. Everything can be fixed or used as parts to fix something else. Perhaps you have the same uncle or grandparent or neighbor that keeps everything or looks at other people's trash on pick up day and if he sees something that interests him, he will take it. Real collecting is more than just being a pack rat. People who collect have a certain drive — a certain need to find just the right piece and when they do, all is right with the world.

There are lots of reasons why people collect. Some people collect as an investment. They look for special items that they know they can make a profit on when they decide that the moment is right to sell. Others collect because they find the same doll that they had when they were little or one that they wanted, but couldn't afford. Perhaps a person finds a tobacco tin that reminds them of the same kind of tobacco that grandpa used before he passed away. There are just about as many reasons why people collect as there are things to collect. However, there are some basic rules for collecting that everyone should follow.

The first rule to collecting is to buy the very best example that you can afford. If you can afford the mint condition *Barbie*®, buy it. If you can't, then try to get the very best that your budget will allow. Then as you get more money, replace those less than perfect examples with better ones. Along those same lines, if you just can't find a mint serving dish to complete your set of Blue Willow dinnerware, then buy the very best serving dish that you can find and that you can afford. Your collection doesn't have to be perfect, but you do want it to be as close to perfect as you can get it.

In order to know whether you have a good example of your collectible, you have to know the standards. That brings us to our second rule of collecting. Know what is considered mint condition for whatever item you choose to collect. Some collectibles are so rare that even a small crack or chip is considered wonderful condition. Once you have determined what experts consider to be the best, use that as your standard when you go hunting for your own pieces.

Third, know the history behind the objects you choose to collect. Just like people, collectibles have a story. Research and find out who made your pieces, what purpose they served, when and where they were made and how. Knowing this information will not only make your collection more valuable if you choose to sell it, it will make your collection more interesting for you. You will appreciate your collection more if you know the effort and care put into your pieces and the story of how they came to be.

Finally, and maybe most importantly, collect what you love. Yes, you can collect items as an investment, but if you go into collecting for that purpose, there is no guarantee that you will ever get the price you want when you decide to sell. It becomes work to collect items just because they are considered hot, and who knows how long that trend will last. What is best for someone else isn't always best for you. Instead, collect things that make you happy, that remind you of good times and good people. In the end you will be happier for it.

Pointers for Displaying Collectibles

For some, the name of the game is the number of items in their collection, sort of like the saying, "The person who dies with the most toys wins." But displaying your collection isn't just about gathering all your pieces together to prove how many examples you have. Most collectors will tell you that it's quality, not quantity that makes a collection special no matter what the focus of your passion. Squeezing all your pieces into one display generally isn't the most appealing way to show off your collection. When there are too many pieces in one place, the truly special items get lost visually in the myriad of examples rather than standing out and making a statement. So you have a wonderful collection and yet you aren't certain how to go about displaying your pieces? Here are some things to keep in mind for creating impressive displays.

SIZE — Size is an important consideration. If you choose objects to display together, it is wise to have differing sizes, but don't choose items that are drastically different so that one large piece completely steals the stage while the other pieces are so small that no one even notices. Think about how florists make flower arrangements. Generally, the flowers aren't all one height, but then again, the florist doesn't use one big sunflower in the middle and stick a bunch of daisies all around the bottom. He or she generally tries to make a more natural transition from large to small.

COLOR — As with creating a decorating scheme for a room or choosing the clothes you wear, color is a consideration when you display your collection. For most collections, try to choose colors in your pieces that complement one another or try choosing all the same color perhaps in different shades. Either of these techniques will give your display a sense of order and that the pieces belong together rather than just throwing something together. There are some cases such as quilts for example where color isn't as much of a consideration.

TEXTURE — Texture can have a very subtle effect on your display. Texture is more than just how something feels to the touch. There's also visual texture. While texture can be a rough surface versus and smooth surface, it can also be a display where some items are long and thin, and others are soft and flowing. Mixing textures helps keep the viewer from getting bored. A simple example is the classic vase of flowers. The vase is a solid object with very distinct lines. The flowers are dynamic, varying from one to the other with different silhouettes.

SCALE — Scale is also an important factor when creating a display. You don't want your display to seem cramped in a space, but you also don't want it floating around without an anchor. An example of the wrong scale would be to put miniature Christmas ornaments on a full-sized tree or vice-versa with full-size bulbs on a miniature tree. The same is true when you choose a display case, curio cabinet, fireplace mantel, etc.

THEME — A theme isn't necessary for a good display, but it can help if you aren't feeling particularly inspired. A theme can be as simple or extravagant as you want it to be. Generally the simpler, the better, but that isn't true across the board. An example of a simple theme would be showing off a special group of coffee grinders amongst other coffee-related items such as a vintage coffee can, a painting of coffee bean fields, and a scale to weigh coffee beans.

PATTERN — Patterns can also help the uninspired. If nothing else, create a pattern of color, size, shape, or type of object. For instance, if you collect a certain type of pottery, interchange bowls and pitchers to form a pattern across the display area. Just try to make sure that they are different enough to be noticeable. In other words don't try to make a pattern of crocks and bowls since they are similarly shaped items and people may not notice the difference or understand what you were trying to accomplish.

Home Furnishings

Art
Arts and Crafts
Boxes
Furniture

The Queen Victoria® Bed and Breakfast Inn

Cape May, New Jersey

Dane and Joan Wells

Arts and Crafts Furniture

© George Gardner

ABOVE: ONE OF THE COUNTRY'S MOST FAMOUS VICTORIAN INNS, THE QUEEN VICTORIA® GREETS GUESTS ON A STUNNINGLY BEAUTIFUL SUMMER DAY.

Welcoming guests since 1980, The Queen Victoria® is one of America's most famous Victorian bed and breakfast inns. Two faithfully restored historic homes offer 21 inviting rooms and suites furnished with fine antiques and handmade quilts including a wonderful collection of Arts and Crafts furniture. The decor is uncluttered in keeping with the Arts and Crafts style and has great attention to detail and many thoughtful extras.

The Queen Victoria® is conveniently located in the center of Cape May's historic district, one block from the Atlantic Ocean, shops and fine restaurants. With quiet classical music in the background, you can relax in the parlor in front of the glowing fireplace. Comfortable reading areas are well stocked with mystery, history, and art books, and British magazines providing a perfect backdrop for quiet conversations with fellow guests. For true Victorian enjoyment, fifty rocking chairs fill porches, gardens and a rooftop sundeck. A wicker swing takes you back to a quieter time.

In 1980, Dane and Joan Wells moved from Philadelphia to purchase one of Cape May's venerable homes, "The Beverly", a summer rooming house complete with 1950s style kitchenettes and a gaggle of roll-away cots. They left behind steady jobs—Dane's as manager of a "Main Street" economic development program for Philadelphia and Joan's as Executive Director of The Victorian Society in America. They opened The Queen Victoria® Bed and Breakfast Inn in the spring of 1981. In 1989, they purchased the rundown rooming house next door and transformed it into Prince Albert Hall, expanding the inn to offer guests more space and amenities. Dane and Joan have diverse backgrounds, which have

© George Gardner

LEFT: A BEAUTIFUL EXAMPLE OF ONE OF THE QUEEN VICTORIA'S® ARTS AND CRAFTS STYLE ROOMS.

© George Gardner

contributed to their skills and expertise as now veteran innkeepers.

The contact with so many guests over the years is one of the best paybacks Dane and Joan Wells have gained as owners of The Queen Victoria®. Their daughter, Elizabeth, put it best one day when she came home from school to discover to her disappointment that a young guest she had enjoyed had left that morning. She looked up at her parents with tears in her eyes and said, "But couldn't we keep just some of them." The Wells explain that's often how they have felt, too. One of the most rewarding aspects of innkeeping has been to have guests return to visit again and again.

LEFT: GUESTS ARE INVITED TO PLAY THEIR FAVORITE TUNES ON THE QUEEN VICTORIA'S® ARTS AND CRAFTS STYLE PIANO.

BELOW: ANOTHER INVITING ARTS AND CRAFTS STYLE ROOM FOR THE QUEEN VICTORIA'S® GUESTS TO ENJOY.

© George Gardner

Arbor Rose
Bed and Breakfast
Stockbridge, Massachusettes
Christina Alsop and Family

Boxes

ABOVE: A BLANKET OF SNOW COVERS THE ARBOR ROSE BED AND BREAKFAST.

As guests approach the front entrance, they come across a rose arbor, which for a brief three weeks starting in late June, is covered with old-fashioned cluster roses. The tendrils wave high in the air and the rockers on the front porch invite guests to sit and relax. Old double French doors stand open inviting guests to enter the polished hallway. Chances are the animals will greet you or you'll hear voices from the kitchen in the back.

In winter, the Franklin woodstove in the front parlor makes for a cozy place to sit especially after a day at the ski slopes. Another option is visit the new Norman Rockwell Museum or the Clark Museum home of one of the nicest collections of American Impressionists. The summer is symphony season and Tanglewood, summer home of the Boston Symphony, is the place to be. Take a picnic under the stars and enjoy your musical evening. But that's not all. Summer is also the time for homemade applesauce and pie with fruit from the orchard, tying herbs in bundles for omelets, going to the numerous flea markets, antique shows, and craft shows, and for taking afternoon naps while the breeze plays with the curtains and the locusts sing in the locust trees. Mountain biking, walking the Appalachian Trail, swimming and tubing on the Green River are just some of the activities for those guests interested in a livelier getaway.

Families are welcome, and for that reason, some of the rooms have an extra bed or two. Suites are also available with connecting rooms. The farmhouse provides the breakfast room, common room and guest rooms. Next door, the old Sawmill has a more historic flare with its post and beam construction, country furnishings and sounds of the flowing stream.

Looking at the handsome residential houses of Yale Hill, it's difficult to believe it was once the manufacturing hub of Stockbridge. But the inn's sawmill, commonly known as the Comstock mill, was used into the 1930s. The mill itself still stands and houses some of the guestrooms within its old post and beam construction. At one time there were five mills on the Kampoosa Brook—the inn's sawmill, a gristmill, a distillery, a woolen factory, a chair factory, and a trip hammer shop. They were built between 1782 and 1822 and all were located within a half mile of the brook. Once owned by the Lakin family, the Alsops have owned the property for 24 years. Christina first became infatuated with the property because of its abandoned mill. The Mill, renovated in 1993, now houses some of the inn's guestrooms in what used to be the machine room and the storage and drying rooms. The Alsops would someday like to resurrect the water wheel.

Country antiques and collectibles are irresistible for Christina. She enjoys finding treasures at the local white elephant sales and auctions and has almost completely furnished the guest rooms with her finds. Boxes have always had a special place in Christina's heart. From small Pennsylvania painted pantry boxes to dovetail trunks, the Arbor Rose Bed and Breakfast has boxes in every room. They are both decorative and functional as they are great storage solutions for people who don't want more modern cabinets and shelves. Christina recently took a class to learn how to make Shaker boxes and intends to make some for the inn.

RIGHT: CHRISTINA'S BOXES ARE BOTH
DECORATIVE AND VERY FUNCTIONAL. THIS TRUNK
IS THE PERFECT UNOBTRUSIVE HIDING PLACE FOR
STORED ITEMS IN THIS GUESTROOM.

BELOW: COLLECTING CAN BE ESPECIALLY FUN IF
YOU TRY TO USE YOUR ITEMS IN NEW WAYS. HERE,
CHRISTINA USED AN OLD TRUNK AS A COFFEE TABLE
AGAIN BENEFITING FROM ITS STORAGE CAPACITY.

INSET: CHRISTINA RECENTLY TOOK A CLASS TO
LEARN HOW TO MAKE SHAKER BOXES SUCH AS
THOSE SHOWN STACKED ON HER ENTERTAINMENT
CENTER.

© Sabine Vollmer von Falken

© Sabine Vollmer von Falken

17

55 East

Annapolis, Maryland
Mat and Patricia Herban

Art

© Celia Pearson

ABOVE: LOVELY FLOWERS GREET GUESTS AS THEY APPROACH THE FRONT ENTRANCE TO 55 EAST BED AND BREAKFAST.

Built in 1860 as a store for John Russell, 55 East Bed and Breakfast was constructed on land purchased from a tract originally owned by Charles Carroll, one of the Maryland signers of the Declaration of Independence. From its doors, guests can see both the Statehouse and the Harbor—two primary influences in the heart of historic Annapolis.

The house is an excellent example of Italianate Revival architecture, distinguished by its bracketed wood cornice and lintels.

Over the years, the building has served as both a private home and a rooming house. When the Herbans bought the house, it was a private residence that had not been updated since the 1960s. The 9-month renovation ended in a beautiful retreat that offers guests comfortable elegance enhanced by the amenities of the twentieth century. The sunny courtyard is a special delight for reading, visiting or quiet meditation—a secluded garden to enjoy the morning paper with breakfast, visit with friends, or steal a few quiet moments.

Mat and Tricia purchased the home because of its strategic location on a quiet residential street in the heart of Annapolis's Historic District. Guests can walk a mere block and a half to the Statehouse, the U.S. Naval Academy, shops, restaurants and the harbor. In addition to its location, the Herbans liked the floor plan of the house, which offered two living rooms and a dining room for guests while still providing extensive room for their private quarters. Finally, Mat and Tricia appreciated the home's proximity to both Washington, D.C. and Baltimore, two major airports, and water.

Annapolis was small enough to make friends and become part of the community and large enough to support a bed and breakfast business.

The Herbans collect art because they both love it. In addition to their collection of 19th and 20th century American graphics, they inherited Tricia's mother's collection of Oriental art that includes 19th century Japanese prints, Chinese embroidery and an intricately knotted robe. All of these artworks are scattered throughout the house, placed according to the colors of the rooms. Each is framed to its best advantage and then placed in a room rather than framing the art to fit the room's color scheme. In fact, the Japanese Room is painted to suit the prints and robe that are displayed there. The Oriental rug and upholstery fabrics were chosen to match the art as well. It is now a space in which to unwind, chat or entertain. The gas fireplace surrounded by an antique New Orleans mantelpiece adds a special touch of warmth, whatever the season.

RIGHT: THIS 1878 OIL PAINTING ON WALNUT PANEL WAS PAINTED BY EUGENE CICERI. TRICIA NOTES THAT SHE ESPECIALLY LIKES THIS ARRANGEMENT BECAUSE IT OFFERS SOMETHING FOR EVERYONE – WOOD, GLASS, BRASS, AND AN OIL PAINTING.

BELOW: THE HERBANS PAINTED THE JAPANESE ROOM TO COMPLEMENT THEIR ART RATHER THAN FINDING ART TO COMPLEMENT THE ROOM. THE ORIENTAL RUG AND UPHOLSTERY PLAY OFF THE JAPANESE PRINTS ABOVE THE FIREPLACE.

© Celia Pearson

© Celia Pearson

Augusta House

Barrington, Massachusetts
Diane Humphrey

Eastlake Furniture

ABOVE: THE WRAP-AROUND PORCH OF AUGUSTA HOUSE IS THE PERFECT PLACE FOR GUESTS TO ENJOY THEIR BREAKFAST ON SUMMER MORNINGS.

The quaint Berkshire town of Great Barrington was incorporated in 1761 and offers plentiful attractions and activities. Augusta House is a charming 1863 Colonial conveniently located on a quiet street in the beautiful hill section of Great Barrington. It is surrounded by other elegant historic homes and is only a few minutes walk from downtown. Barrington is part of the Berkshires in Western Massachusetts and is a favorite winter ski area for New York City and Boston. The summer offers the Tanglewood Music Festival, Berkshire Botanical Gardens, the Norman Rockwell Museum and much, much more.

On fine summer mornings, a table adorned with fresh flowers awaits guests on the large wrap-around porch. The porch is perfect for relaxing and socializing any time. Overhead is a 200 year old Copper Beech tree, which snuggles near the house. On cooler days, breakfast is served in the common room in the glow of a crystal chandelier with the fireplace blazing.

A massage therapist for over 15 years and a grief counselor, Diane knew she had found her calling to be an innkeeper one day as she herself was enjoying an elegant breakfast at an inn. She then began to read books and talk to numerous innkeepers to learn about the business of innkeeping and how to set up a bed and breakfast. Though it took time, Diane found the perfect house for her purpose. Augusta House is furnished with family heirlooms and the treasures of 20 years of antique- and collectibles-hunting including her collection of dolls and Eastlake furniture. This style of furniture was created by Charles Locke Eastlake and is made of carved wood with fabric upholstery. Mr. Eastlake published *Hints on Household Taste* in England in 1868, and in 1872, the first American edition appeared. It had widespread influence in the states and was illustrated in *The House Beautiful*, published in New York in 1878.

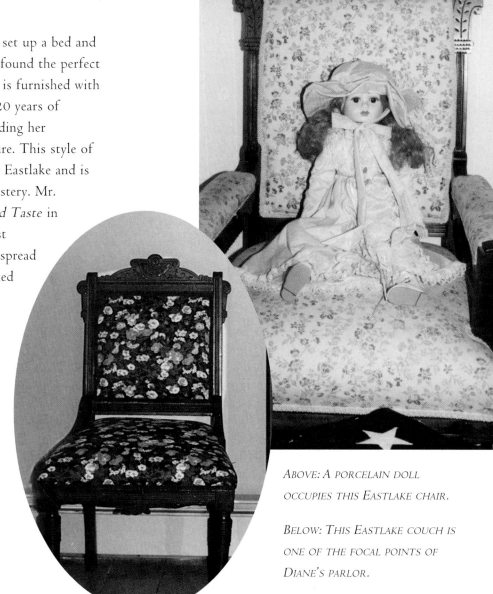

RIGHT: ANOTHER EXAMPLE OF DIANE'S EASTLAKE FURNITURE UPHOLSTERED IN A DARK FABRIC WITH VIBRANT FLOWERS. SOMETIMES REUPHOLSTERING CAN BRING BACK A DAMAGED PIECE, BUT TYPICALLY REFURBISHING ANTIQUES DEVALUES THE PIECE. CHECK WITH AN EXPERT BEFORE YOU REFURBISH FURNITURE.

ABOVE: A PORCELAIN DOLL OCCUPIES THIS EASTLAKE CHAIR.

BELOW: THIS EASTLAKE COUCH IS ONE OF THE FOCAL POINTS OF DIANE'S PARLOR.

Housewares

Books
Clocks
Coffee Grinders
Crocks
Napkin Rings
Pewter
Plates
Railroad Items
Saucers
Teacups
Teapots

Waterloo Country Inn
Princess Anne, Maryland
Erwin and Theresa Kraemer

Coffee Grinders

ABOVE LEFT: ONCE A BRICK PLANTATION HOUSE, THE WATERLOO IS A FULLY RESTORED PRE-REVOLUTIONARY WATERFRONT ESTATE.

INSET: THIS COFFEE GRINDER IS INTERESTING BECAUSE IT HANGS ON THE WALL UNLIKE TRADITIONAL ANTIQUE COFFEE GRINDERS.

Built by a prominent Somerset County landowner, Henry Waggaman, this pre-Revolutionary waterfront estate is a fully restored, historic 1750s gem. Restoration began in 1995 to the mansion and since 1996 the Waterloo has been an elegant country inn. Listed in the National Register of Historic Places, Waterloo is a highly significant brick plantation house. The three-story Flemish bond brick mansion is distinguished by glazed header checkerboard patterns and distinctive quoins on three principal corners. In the nineteenth century, several prominent local families owned the property until 1864, when the Somerset County government purchased this Georgian style house for use as an almshouse. The county retained ownership of the Monie Creek property until 1948 when Waterloo once again became the property of a private owner.

The Waterloo Country Inn is situated on a tidal pond, a paradise for nature lovers. Guests may stroll through the beautiful gardens and the majestic forest with its wide variety of trees and shrubs, some of which are rare to the area. The inn's location with its elegant lodgings and peaceful ambience make the Waterloo the ideal and perfect get-away, but it is also just a short drive from Ocean City, Maryland and Delaware Coastal Resort regions.

While visiting the Eastern Shore of Maryland as tourists from Switzerland, Erwin and Theresa discovered Waterloo, a stately manor house. The

Kraemers fell in love with the estate immediately and within a few days, decided to change their lives to include this wonderful manor. Erwin had been an executive director at a well-known electric company, and Theresa had a managing position with Zurich Bank, but within a year, both made arrangements to move from Zurich, Switzerland, to the Eastern Shore in August 1995.

The renovation began just one month later in September 1995. The Kraemers confronted several difficulties while restoring one of the most treasured landmarks on Maryland's Eastern Shore. Neither Erwin nor Theresa knew much about the laws and restrictions of the States, but with the help of other area entrepreneurs, they opened the Waterloo just 9 months later in June 1996.

Erwin and Theresa's coffee grinder collection grew out of a fascination for the different kinds of mechanisms involved as well as the different countries and histories of each. They display their coffee grinders mostly in the dining areas of Waterloo. They also have a collection of clocks that they enjoy sharing with guests.

ABOVE: THESE ARE JUST A FEW EXAMPLES OF THE KRAEMER'S MORE TRADITIONAL COFFEE GRINDERS.

THE DINING ROOM MANTEL IS HOME TO THIS SELECTION OF COFFEE GRINDERS. A BEAUTIFUL CLOCK FROM THE KRAEMER'S CLOCK COLLECTION HANGS ABOVE.

Inn at Norwood

Sykesville, Maryland
Kelly and Steve Crum

Teapots and Teacups

Centrally located in the heart of Historic Sykesville, Maryland, the Inn at Norwood is a Colonial Revival home retaining much of its original charm. The inn was built in 1906 by the architect J.H. Fowble as his family's residence. Mr. Fowble built many of the other buildings in the town of Sykesville as well. Guests may choose to relax on the front porch overlooking the town, or just snuggle up in the parlor with a good book.

On the National Register of Historic Places, the quaint town of Sykesville is named for James Sykes who purchased the land from George Patterson. The town's completely restored railroad station was originally built in 1884 but is now a restaurant. Sykesville has much to offer: great restaurants, a museum, many festivals throughout the year, hiking and biking trails, fishing, antique shops and much more.

ABOVE LEFT: THE INN AT NORWOOD IS A CHARMING EXAMPLE OF COLONIAL REVIVAL ARCHITECTURE ESPECIALLY WHEN SURROUNDED BY FALL FOLIAGE.

INSET: MANY COLLECTORS PREFER TO USE THEIR COLLECTIBLES. THE CRUMS USE THIS FLORAL TEAPOT TO SERVE TEA TO THE INN'S GUESTS.

The idea of becoming bed and breakfast owners came about in Kelly and Stevon's first year of dating. They traveled to different bed and breakfasts each month for a romantic getaway. Kelly and Stevon fell in love with the concept — the people they met and the food they enjoyed were fabulous. They took all the things they loved from each bed and breakfast and incorporated it into the Inn at Norwood. Stevon and Kelly Crum along with Kelly's mom, Eva, opened the Inn at Norwood on June 2, 2001. About to retire from her full-time job, Eva wanted something fun to do with her free time. Among other things, Eva loves to decorate and make crafts as well as refinishing furniture. Many of the things in the house are a product of Eva's work.

Stevon always wanted to refurbish an old home and this Colonial Revival was the perfect house — everything needed to be redone. Guests are invited to see the before and after photos. The transformation is unbelievable. Kelly and Stevon each have full-time jobs in addition to running the inn. Kelly is a Finance Director of a Fortune 500 company, and Stevon owns several carpet cleaning businesses. Kelly's mom, Eva, enjoys her retirement job of running the inn as well as managing and stocking an onsite country store called "Eve's Place."

ABOVE: SCALE IS AN IMPORTANT CONSIDERATION WHEN DECIDING HOW TO DISPLAY YOUR COLLECTIBLES. THESE DAINTY TEACUPS WOULD GET LOST IN A LARGE DISPLAY CASE.

BELOW: THE CRUMS UTILIZE THE AREA ABOVE THEIR KITCHEN CABINETS TO DISPLAY THEIR TEAPOTS AND TEACUPS AS WELL.

Inn at Stockbridge

Stockbridge, Massachusetts
Len and Alice Schiller

Pewter

ABOVE: THE INN AT STOCKBRIDGE IS A GEORGIAN-STYLED HOME CONSIDERED A SUMMER RESIDENCE BY ITS FIRST OWNER, A BOSTON ATTORNEY.

Located in the Massachusetts Berkshires, the Inn at Stockbridge is set far back from the road on 12 secluded acres just one mile from downtown. The inn is a turn-of-the-century Georgian-style country inn built in 1906 by Philip Blagdon, a Boston attorney. He considered the house a summer residence and a summer cottage. The land was originally owned by his wife's family, the Runnels, but it can be traced back to the original settlers in Stockbridge, a missionary family by the name of Williams, who came to the area in 1739 to convert the Stockbridge Native Americans to Christianity. The house remained in the Blagdon family until the 1970s. After being a guesthouse for a short time under the ownership of Karen Putman, Don and Lee Weitz bought the Inn in 1982 and lovingly restored it adding some personal space and building a terrace room. They named it the Inn at Stockbridge. In 1995, current owners, Len and Alice Schiller, bought the inn moving from Maplewood, New Jersey and making Stockbridge their home. It had only 8 rooms at that time, but with the desire to meet guest demand for more amenities including fireplaces and whirlpools, Len and Alice built the Cottage house suites in 1997 and the Barn suites in 2001. The Inn now has 16 well-appointed guestrooms meeting the demand for comfortable luxury.

A great inn is a captivating combination of wonderful guests, a gracious staff, magical surroundings, delicious foods, and luxurious rooms. Len and Alice pride themselves on the peaceful charm and elegance of their inn. Alice is primarily responsible for the comfortable elegance including the pewter collection on display from the previous owners. Len and Alice combined their personal collection with that of the previous owners to create a wonderful display of plates, cups, bowls, and mugs. The theme and colors of the dining room was created around the pewter. One consideration was the silver in the toile wall coverings.

ABOVE: LEN AND ALICE COMBINED THEIR COLLECTION WITH THAT OF THE PREVIOUS OWNERS TO CREATE AN IMPRESSIVE DISPLAY. THE PLATES, CUPS, BOWLS AND MUGS ARE DISPLAYED ON A SIMPLE WHITE SHELF THAT UTILIZES THE OFTEN-UNUSED AREA OVER THE WINDOWS.

INSET: THE THEME AND COLORS OF THE DINING ROOM WERE CREATED AROUND THE PEWTER COLLECTION. THE SILVER TOILE WALL COVERING AND THE WINDOW TREATMENTS WERE CONCEIVED TO ENHANCE THE PEWTER'S COLOR AND SIMPLE DESIGN.

Another Idea

Any collectible that you can trace to its original owner has more market value. Here bed and breakfast owner Barbara Mahoney of The Parsonage on the Green shows off her collection of a child's pewter tea set. It was owned by her grandmother who is pictured in the photograph. An arrangement showing the original owner is very appealing.

The window treatments were also conceived to enhance the pewter. Len and Alice also have an ongoing teapot and teacup collection. They even have a "teacup fountain" displayed in the library. Early morning coffee is served each morning on an antique cherry breakfront and a collection of antique teacups is displayed for the guests. After that, guests can go about their day knowing that they will be welcomed home in the evening by a wonderfully gracious and serene inn.

Bittersweet Farm
Millersburg, Ohio
Norman and MaryLou Crowe

Crocks and Pantry Boxes

ABOVE: THE MAIN HOUSE OF BITTERSWEET FARM IS A NEWLY CONSTRUCTED 1800S HOUSE CREATED FROM PLANS SIMILAR TO A HOME IN CONNECTICUT AND BUILT BY THE OWNERS' AMISH FRIENDS.

Bittersweet Farm is a collage of restored buildings combined with a newly reproduced 1800s house built from plans similar to a home in Connecticut. The main house sits atop the 190-acre farm and has a breathtaking view. Aided by friends from the Amish community, Norm and MaryLou used reclaimed old barn lumber to mill for the floors, ceilings, wall, and trim. A local mason built the stone fireplace, and the bake oven has two cranes that allow for hearthside cooking. It's the perfect place to enjoy a cup of hot cider.

In addition to the two guestrooms in the main house, Norm and MaryLou have also restored a number of old outbuildings and have turned them into cottages to rent. The Crowes love frequent local auctions and sales, so it is only natural that they furnished both the Main House and the cottages with antiques that they have collected over the last 30 years.

Along with the main house and cottages, Norm and

MaryLou also restored a 100-year old barn in which they sell herbs, dried flowers, antiques and collectibles. They grow and harvest all the herbs and flowers themselves in their perennial garden, which is an absolute delight for the senses. These herbs and flowers are then harvested to create beautiful arrangements and wreaths so that visitors can take the country charm of Bittersweet Farm to their own homes. Lectures and tours of the garden are given in which visitors and groups can learn about planning, planting, harvesting and drying flowers and herbs as well as which plants are edible, how to cook with herbs and flowers, and how to make wreaths, potpourri and sachets for decorating. But the Crowes didn't just stop at raising wildflowers and herbs. They also raise peacocks and own chickens that provide farm fresh eggs for breakfast. Guests most certainly enjoy sweet dreams and delicious country breakfasts when they stay it this old fashioned bed and breakfast.

ABOVE RIGHT: THIS COUNTRY PANTRY HOUSES
MANY OF MARYLOU'S CROCKS AND PANTRY
BOXES, MOST IN SHADES OF BLUE. THE OPEN
SHELVES ALLOW THE ITEMS TO BE ENJOYED
RATHER THAN HID AWAY BEHIND CABINET
DOORS.

RIGHT: MARYLOU EVEN HAS MINIATURE
VERSIONS OF HER COUNTRY CROCKS. SHE HAS
TAKEN THE SCALE OF THIS PARTICULAR
COLLECTION INTO CONSIDERATION BY PLACING
THEM IN THIS SMALL SHELVING UNIT WITH
OTHER MINIATURE ITEMS RATHER THAN TRYING
TO DISPLAY THEM WITH THEIR LARGER
COUNTERPARTS.

The Parsonage on the Green

Lee, Massachusetts

Don and Barbara Mahony

Teapots and Teacups

ABOVE: PARSONAGE ON THE GREEN BED AND BREAKFAST HOUSE WAS ORIGINALLY BUILT IN 1851 FOR THE MINISTER OF THE ADJACENT CHURCH, FIRST CONGREGATIONAL CHURCH OF LEE, AT A COST OF ONLY $3,000.

The Parsonage on the Green is located in the downtown historic section of the Village of Lee, Massachusetts. It is situated on the village green, immediately adjacent to the First Congregational Church. The church is one of the most beautiful and historic buildings in the area and boasts the tallest wooden steeple in New England (some say in all the USA). Built for the church in 1851, the house was indeed the parsonage until the 1970s when the church sold the property.

Nestled amid the towering evergreens and maples, The Parsonage on the Green is a three-storied modified center-hall colonial. Its 10-foot ceilings and center hall staircase with carvings make this house a colonial jewel. Elegant in every way, it also gives guests a feeling of home. The house contains an abundance of family heirlooms including photographs and other personal memorabilia that spans generations. In addition, the downtown area of Lee's main street looks like something out of a Norman Rockwell painting, quite possible considering the inn is just minutes from the Norman Rockwell Museum.

The Mahony family lived in Setauket, New York for 31 years. In 1996, they visited the Berkshires on Yom Kippur. Don remarked how he had forgotten how beautiful the Berkshires were. Barbara had always wanted to operate a bed and breakfast after retiring from teaching. By April 1997, the Mahonys owned The Parsonage on the Green. Don retired in January 1997, and Barbara in June 1997. They opened the inn for business over the July Fourth weekend that very year.

Barbara didn't begin her collection of teacups on her own. Until 1970, she didn't even enjoy a cup of tea. It all started for Barbara when her mother gave her matching sets of teacups and dessert plates as gifts for graduating from college and at Christmas. Those pieces were special because Barbara's mother, Friederike Steigmeyer Armitage, inherited them from her mother Alice Engelhard Steigmeyer. Then during the 1970s, Barbara found that she actually liked tea and began attending tea demonstrations and collecting teapots.

The teapots and teacups are used in decorating in the library, parlor, and dining room. They can be found in the upstairs hall on an antique doll's table as well as in china cabinets in the dining area. Although the collection is displayed throughout the inn as part of the décor, Barbara does use them for tea time with the guests as well. "Tea time at The Parsonage is a ritual that invites relaxation and enjoyment," says Barbara.

ABOVE: THESE BLUE WILLOW DOLL DISHES WERE BARBARA'S WHEN SHE WAS A CHILD. THEY ARE ON DISPLAY ON A SHELF ABOVE THE DINING ROOM WINDOW.

INSET BELOW: THIS TEAPOT IS VILLEROY AND BOCH VIEUX LUXEMBOURG VITRO PORCELAIN. HER HUSBAND BOUGHT IT ON A TRIP TO GERMANY IN 1981 TO ACCOMPANY HER ROYAL COPENHAGEN CHINA.

LEFT: BARBARA'S SET OF ROYAL COPENHAGEN CHINA IS DISPLAYED ON TOP OF HER CHINA CABINET IN THE DINING ROOM.

The Villa Bed and Breakfast

Tacoma, Washington
Greg and Becky Anglemyer

Napkin Rings

The historic mansion features elegant Palladian windows that lighten the interior even on winter's dreariest days. Filled with vibrant colors and beautiful art, The Villa embodies the warmth and charm of Italy. One of the best things about owning an "Italian" home is that the Italians are some of the world's greatest collectors. This has enabled Greg and Becky to use an eclectic mix of fine décor from around the globe to achieve a feel that is both luxurious and comfortable. The mood is definitely "Italian country." And fortunately, Becky's napkin ring collection has grown over the years to the size that it can adequately handle the eight to twelve guests that they host each day.

Greg and Becky purchased The Villa in 1994 with the intent of opening their first bed and breakfast. Their interest started about 15 years earlier during their first stay at a B&B. One of the many fine touches they admired about the bed and breakfast in which they stayed was a set of napkin rings that looked like ladies wearing ball gowns. The upper torso was china and placing the napkin through the ring created the gown. Enchanted by their experience there, Greg and Becky began plotting their eventual escape from their corporate lives. Since Greg would still keep his corporate job for a few years, it was necessary that he be able to commute to Seattle. They were fortunate to discover the Stadium Historic District in Tacoma, Washington. The area's lovely architecture was a diverse mix of styles— a perfect "escape" even for locals.

Becky also started hunting for the napkin rings that so impressed her. She assumed they were from England, but after a long search, she discovered that they were in

ABOVE: FILLED WITH VIBRANT COLORS AND BEAUTIFUL ART, THE VILLA EMBODIES THE WARMTH AND CHARM OF ITALY EVEN ON WINTER'S DREARIEST DAYS.

BELOW: ONE OF BECKY'S MORE TRADITIONAL NAPKIN RINGS.

fact antebellum American and very rare. While browsing antique stores, she began to notice that there were a number of figurines that have holes in them, and a napkin could be easily tucked in them. Thus began the collection.

Becky started with figurines: horses, deer, people and birds. Then she decided that small pitchers and vases could have a napkin end stuck into them. Finding the right size, with an appropriately-sized hole or some other means of holding a napkin is the challenge. "The fun is shopping for them—you never know what shelf they will be hiding on," Becky explains. She now owns several dozen, allowing her to choose colors or styles to match whatever she has planned for the table décor each day. Many times the first conversation around the table involves villa guests showing off their particular napkin ring. Sometimes they even choose where they are going to sit based on the figurine that is there!

RIGHT: BECKY SHOWS HOW NON-TRADITIONAL ITEMS CAN BE USED AS NAPKIN RINGS.

BELOW: AN ARRAY OF NON-TRADITIONAL NAPKIN RINGS THAT BECKY USES. GUESTS FIND THEM VERY INTERESTING AND THEY ARE OFTEN GREAT CONVERSATION STARTERS AROUND THE BREAKFAST TABLE.

35

Acacia House

Fairmont, West Virginia
George and Kathy Sprowls

Saucers and Plates

Located on Locust Avenue, Acacia House derives its name from the surrounding locust trees. The Locust tree is a member of the Acacia family. Built in 1917 for T.L. Burchinal, superintendent of construction for the Marion County Court House, the four-story-brown brick home features beautiful oak woodwork throughout and six decorative fireplaces.

Guests may partake in numerous activities including hiking mountain trails or just relaxing on the inviting glass-enclosed front porch. "This is your time to spend doing exactly what you want," say innkeepers George and Kathy.

Throughout the house, the rooms are tastefully decorated with antiques and collectibles, some of which are tagged for sale. Or guests may spend a little time in the one-room antique shop where they just may find that special something they've always "needed."

Experience the charm of small town, USA, where people are friendly and sociable. The architecture of the late 1800s and early 1900s lures people to the downtown Fairmont area just minutes away from the inn by foot. The walk around town is quiet now, but that wasn't the case when Confederate leaders chose to pursue Union troops and confiscate supplies in the spring of 1863 just a short distance from the bed and breakfast. Known as the Jones's Raid, General John D. Imboden and General William E. Jones designed a raid to destroy portions of the B&O Railroad and break up the restored government of Virginia. After failing to destroy the B&O line at Rowlesburg, the two men destroyed the bridge at Fairmont. However, after several weeks, the Jones-Imboden Raid failed to destroy significant portions of the B&O or break up the restored government of Virginia.

ABOVE: THE FOUR-STORY BROWN BRICK BED AND BREAKFAST IS NAMED FOR THE SURROUNDING LOCUST TREES THAT ARE MEMBERS OF THE ACACIA FAMILY.

George was the Naval attaché in Cairo, Egypt, before, during and after the Gulf War. Kathy was looking for something to do that would allow her to work on her own, be flexible, and not be responsible to any boss for when George retired. The Sprowls lived in representational housing in both Riyadh, Saudi Arabia, and in Cairo, and oftentimes had houseguests, some of whom were rather high ranking. After this experience, they decided they liked this style of living enough to make it a paying proposition. When George retired in 1991, he asked where Kathy would like to go. Since she had followed him everywhere as a Navy wife, Kathy got to decide where the business would be. They decided it was time to return home to West Virginia though they were originally from the Wheeling/Wellsburg area in the Northern Panhandle. George returned to school to get his Ph.D., and Kathy opened the inn and antique shop.

Kathy has collected most of her life. Growing up, she always had marbles, or dishes, or books that she collected, none of which have survived, unfortunately. Kathy also had a love of pretty glass and often went to her local "dump" area to hunt for "treasures," and says that she often found them. Things haven't changed much over the years. Kathy loves everything she collects and displays everything to be enjoyed by her family, friends, and guests. In fact, her 4 and 7-year old grandchildren appreciate mee-maw's collections. They are allowed to touch anything and everything BUT with one finger only. This method works! They, too, are starting their own collections.

RIGHT: THESE SMALL SAUCERS ARE GROUPED IN A SMALL DECORATIVE SHELVING UNIT.

BELOW: A SHELF MADE OF MODELING ENCIRCLES THE ENTIRE DINING ROOM. KATHY DISPLAYS AN EXTENSIVE COLLECTION OF PLATES INCLUDING THIS SECTION WITH THEMED PLATES.

Fitch Hill Inn Bed and Breakfast

Hyde Park, Vermont

Gary and Sharon Coquillette

Railroad Dinnerware

ABOVE: THE FITCH HILL INN IN ITS CHRISTMAS FINERY IS A BEAUTIFUL PLACE TO SPEND THE HOLIDAYS.

Approximately 200 years old, the Fitch Hill Inn is a farmhouse built by Darius Fitch after his marriage in 1797. The son of one of Hyde Park's "founding fathers," the house remained in the Fitch family for four generations until it finally was passed out of the family in the mid 1900s. Although most of the surrounding farmland was sold for development, the house remained a family home, with a long-term apartment rental in the annex addition, until the mid-1980s when the bed and breakfast was started. The house, began as a simple Federal style home, but was renovated in the mid to late 1800s to a more Victorian style house by adding bay windows and a porch with gingerbread trim. Between 1965 and 1975, the owners at the time made several modifications to the interior of the house, including building bookshelves on either side of the bay window in the living room and closing off the doorways to the two parlors building a niche with shelves into one of them. Much of the displayed collection is housed in these two areas.

Gary and Sharon purchased the Fitch Hill Inn in June of 2000 after a two-and-a-half-year search for the right bed and breakfast. Originally from Cedar Rapids, Iowa, Sharon was a teacher for visually-impaired students, and Gary was working maintenance at the same education agency. They felt that the Midwest wasn't the best location for a year-round bed and breakfast, so they initially looked for their ideal house in Colorado. However, the prices there were less than ideal, and they began to look elsewhere. Because of their love of the changing seasons and the mountains, Gary and

Sharon chose to look in New England, and Vermont seemed like a logical choice.

Gary and Sharon's railroad collection, some of which is displayed in the inn, started out as a plan to purchase "a few" railroad items to decorate the bar Gary was building in their Iowa basement. Both had relatives (great grandfathers and great uncles) who had worked for various railroads, and they enjoyed riding the various scenic railroads across the country. They began with a few lanterns, glassware, and other railroad memorabilia that they thought would be an interesting and appropriate theme for a bar area. Of course, those with the collecting bug can't just stop at a few decorative items, and they were soon hooked. Gary and Sharon decided to narrow their railroad collecting primarily to china, silverware, playing cards, travel brochures, and items from the Waterloo, Cedar Falls and Northern RR (WCF&N) where Gary's uncle was station master. They specifically collect small oval platters of various patterns and all pieces of the "Glory of the West" pattern from the Great Northern RR.

Because the cards and brochures do not display easily (or stand up to handling), they are not currently displayed in the inn. However, Gary and Sharon do use the china and the WCF&N items in the dining room

ABOVE: BUILT-IN CABINETS ON BOTH SIDES OF THE COMMON ROOM'S FRONT WINDOW DISPLAYS GARY AND SHARON'S COLLECTION OF VARIOUS CHINA FROM THE WATERLOO, CEDAR FALLS AND NORTHERN RAILROAD (WCF&N) WHERE GARY'S UNCLE WAS STATIONMASTER.

INSET: GARY AND SHARON ALSO COLLECT TRAVEL BROCHURES, PHOTOS AND OTHER PAPER PARAPHERNALIA. BECAUSE THEY DO NOT HOLD UP TO HANDLING, THEY ARE DISPLAYED IN FRAMES, AND MANY ARE NOT DISPLAYED IN THE INN.

RIGHT: A DOOR-SIZED NICHE IN THE WALL IS TRIMMED WITH MOLDING TO MATCH THAT AROUND THE ACTUAL DOORS BUT IS ONLY DEEP ENOUGH TO DISPLAY GARY AND SHARON'S GLASSWARE ALONG WITH A FEW OTHER ITEMS OF SIMILAR SIZE.

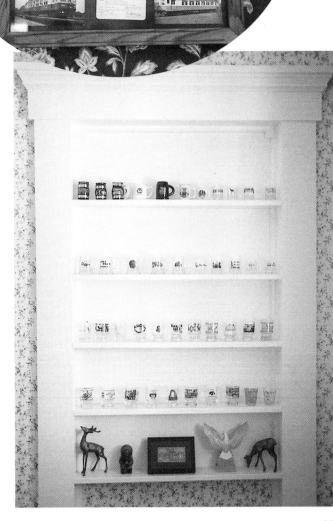

and living room. Many of the small oval platters are on plate racks hung on the dining room walls. The rest of them, along with the Great Northern items and various other railroad pieces that had graced the bar in Iowa are displayed on the bookshelves in the living room. The WCF&N items are in their own small wall display case nearby.

Lynn's Inn
Flagstaff, Arizona
Bob and Linda Gray

Rare Books

ABOVE LEFT: "THE OLD ENGLAND HOUSE" IS WITHOUT QUESTION THE FINEST AND ONLY RESIDENTIAL EXAMPLE OF BEVELED HAND-CUT SANDSTONE ARCHITECTURE IN FLAGSTAFF.

INSET: INSTEAD OF SHEET MUSIC, BOB AND LINDA'S PIANO HOLDS AN EYE-CATCHING BOOK. SEVERAL OTHERS ARE POSITIONED ON TOP OF THE PIANO IN A SYMMETRICAL DESIGN.

"The Old England House," now Lynn's Inn, is one of Flagstaff's remaining mansions from the turn-of-the-century and is on the National Register of Historic Places. It's a unique historical bed and breakfast within walking distance of Flagstaff's Main Street Historic district. Built in 1902, the homestead style inn is built of sandstone excavated from a local quarry by the England family. This beautiful two-story Victorian era home has been opening its doors to travelers and visitors since 1998 when the Gray's opened its antique doors to the public. Up until that time, it had always been a private residence. It is without question, the finest and only residential example of hand-cut beveled sandstone architecture in Flagstaff.

When the Gray's considered opening a bed and breakfast in Flagstaff, they knew that the England house was the only house with enough appeal architecturally and historically to consider developing. Having been on the back burner for about 19 years, the Gray's finally decided the time was right and purchased "The Old England House."

Both innkeepers have a love for antiques, auctions and collectibles. One of their most treasured collections is that of their rare books. "I thoroughly enjoy the never-ending stream of interesting travelers that are drawn to bed and breakfasts. They come from all over the world so there is a lot of interaction and dialogue concerning our rare book collection," says Linda.

The collection began as a means to read history books written at the time of their particular contents—an effort to get inside the thinking of another time and age. Part of the collection is the focal point of the parlor and is displayed in an old English hutch. The collection itself ranges from 1600 to the present. There are small stacks or lines of books in each room accompanied by a pair of antique bookends.

The inn is located at the turn to the Grand Canyon, and is directly on the road leading to Lowell Observatory where the planet Pluto was discovered. Whether the desire is for peaceful relaxation with a good book, or an adventurous trip down the white water rapids of the Colorado River, Bob and Linda Gray are ready to make each night at the inn a welcome homecoming. Their motto is "Lynn's Inn, a celebration of life!"

ABOVE: THIS OLD ENGLISH HUTCH IS THE FOCAL POINT OF THE PARLOR AND CONTAINS PART OF BOB AND LINDA'S COLLECTION OF RARE BOOKS.

LEFT: A TRANSOM OVER ONE OF THE DOORS CONTAINS A DECORATIVE DISPLAY CONSISTING OF A WATERING CAN, IVY AND A STACK OF BOOKS.

Pottery
and Glass

Bottles
Cobalt Glassware
Danish Porcelain
Fire King Dishes
Hand-Painted Dishes
Pottery
Wedgwood
Yellow Ware

The Golden Pheasant

Erwinna, Pennsylvania

Michel and Barbara Faure

Quimper Pottery

The Golden Pheasant Inn is situated on the eastern boundary of Tinicum Township between the Delaware River and Canal. This section of Bucks County was originally called Manor of Highlands. In 1699, the London Company purchased the 7,500 acres from William Penn. With the completion of the northern leg of the Delaware Canal in 1832, oases sprang up along the canal to serve the canal men on their runs from Easton to Bristol. The Delaware House was built in 1857 as a stop for a change of mules, beer, salt cakes, and a bed for the night. Over the years, it had many owners and its name was changed to the Golden Pheasant Inn. Built of local fieldstone, the inn features exposed stone walls, recessed windows, beamed ceilings and an original tap room.

Following the family tradition of Provincial France, Barbara and Michel Faure, with their five daughters, became resident proprietors of the inn in 1986. The Golden Pheasant Inn continues to service travelers with food and lodging. Romantic lodging is available in six beautifully restored guestrooms with canopy beds and fireplaces. Creative French cuisine by Chef Michel, a native of Grenoble, France, is served in three traditionally restored dining rooms including the Tavern with its fireplace, the Blaise Room with beamed ceiling and the candle lighted Greenhouse overlooking the canal. The inn is 13 miles north of New Hope, Pennsylvania, and close to beautiful parks, scenic roads and quaint covered bridges. Designated as an historic building and listed on

ABOVE: THE GOLDEN PHEASANT IS PARTICULARLY ALLURING AT SUNSET.

the National Register of Historic Places, the inn is 60 miles from Philadelphia or New York City. Through the years, each of the daughters has worked at the inn. Today Brittany and Blake assist their father in the kitchen and maintain the gardens. Brook and Blaise assist their mother in managing the guestrooms and restaurant.

Barbara Faure collects and sells Quimper Pottery at the inn. Pronounced "kem-pair," Quimper, France, has been a pottery town since it was occupied by the Roman Empire. Eventually settled by Celts, Brittany Province did not officially become part of France until 1532, thus retaining its Celtic heritage. Quimper Pottery is famous for its faience, which is glazed pottery with highly colored hand-painted decoration. The current history of Quimper pottery began in 1690 with the

44

arrival of Jean-Baptiste Bousquet. Utilitarian pottery such as tablewares and clay pipes for smoking tobacco were his specialty. By 1708, his son Pierre took over the firm and expanded operations. Chinese porcelain was difficult for French noblemen to obtain, so they sought faience as a more available option to silver and gold tableware. Given the time span, over three hundred years, today's collector has an incredible range of work from which to choose.

Both the Tavern and Blaise Room at the inn are accented with copper pots and Barbara's collection of Quimper Pottery. Her private collection is featured on walls, shelves, and windowsills. The dining tables feature Quimper candlesticks, flower vases, plates, and animals that are available for purchase, the favorite being the Breton truffle pig.

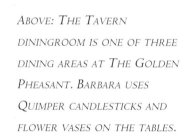

ABOVE: THE TAVERN DININGROOM IS ONE OF THREE DINING AREAS AT THE GOLDEN PHEASANT. BARBARA USES QUIMPER CANDLESTICKS AND FLOWER VASES ON THE TABLES.

INSET: BARBARA DISPLAYS PART OF HER QUIMPER COLLECTION IN A WALL CABINET AND OTHERS ARE HUNG DIRECTLY ON THE WALL.

LEFT: THE BLAISE ROOM IS ALSO ACCENTED WITH BARBARA'S QUIMPER COLLECTION. SHE USES THE COLORFUL PIECES ON THE WALLS, WINDOWSILLS, AND ON THE TABLES.

Photo courtesy of Diane Monelli.

LEFT: WHO COULD RESIST THE WELCOMING ENTRANCE TO THE DEERHILL INN WITH ITS FLOWERS AND CLIMBING VINES?

The Deerhill Inn

West Dover, Vermont

Michael and Linda Anelli

Yellow Ware Pottery

BELOW: LINDA DECORATES HER KITCHEN BY OPENING THE DOORS TO HER HOOSIER TO DISPLAY HER EXTENSIVE COLLECTION OF YELLOW WARE. HUTCHES, HOOSIERS, AND ARMOIRES ARE ALL EXCELLENT PLACES TO SHOW OFF YOUR COLLECTIBLES WITHOUT PUTTING THEM IN A FORMAL DISPLAY CASE.

Located in the Deerfield Valley of Vermont, the Deerhill Inn is the perfect backdrop for relaxation in every season. In the winter, ski at some of the East's best resorts. Cross-country trails on the inn's perimeter link up with some of the finest touring centers in Vermont. In spring, maple fills the air as sugaring starts, gardens flourish and the mountains become green again after the long winter's nap. In summer, fishing and golfing are available for the sporting types, or there's the Marlboro Music Festival for those who enjoy the arts. And in the fall . . . well, Mother Nature speaks for herself and always dazzles even the most jaded wanderers with her beauty.

From the time you arrive and first glimpse the panoramic views of the Green Mountains, the Deerhill Inn will continually take your breath away. Relearn what it means to relax. Put your feet up. While away the hours in one of the 15 guestrooms, all with private baths and comfortable appointments. Linger in the living room by the fireplace or curl up in the library with a good book. But whatever you choose, please don't rush.

At sunset enjoy a cordial and conversation on the patio or in the lounge. Make a new friend. Renew an old love. Bring back old memories or create new ones. Then move into the dining rooms—a crackling fire, hand painted murals, and inspiring vistas. The menu is a sampling of imaginative country cuisine, executed with flair and enthusiasm by Chef Michael. It is complemented by an unusual and creative wine list, featuring wines from North and South America.

Michael and Linda collect yellow ware pottery. Yellow ware has become a popular collectible in recent years spurred in part by the attention it has received from several home shows. Established as a transitional ware between primitive redware and more formal chinas, yellow ware was produced primarily in England where the clays produced the warm tones of the pottery and was highly utilitarian in its usage surviving many years of usage in the everyday home.

Photo courtesy of William Hurd.

ABOVE: *THIS DISTRESSED FREESTANDING CABINET HAS PART OF LINDA'S COLLECTION ARRANGED ON TOP.*

LEFT: *LINDA UTILIZES EVERY PART OF HER KITCHEN TO DISPLAY HER COLLECTIBLES. HERE YOU CAN SEE THAT SHE DISPLAYS HER YELLOW WARE ON TOP OF HER KITCHEN CABINETS, ON HER COUNTERTOP, AND EVEN ON A SHELF OVER THE SLIDING GLASS DOOR. SHE ALSO USES HER YELLOW WARE TO SERVE GUESTS.*

Desert Dove

Tucson, Arizona
Harvey and Betty Ross

Watt Pottery

Located in Tucson, Arizona on four acres, the Desert Dove is nestled in the foothills of the Rincon Mountains near Saguaro National Park East. You will feel right at home in this natural sun-baked adobe bed and breakfast. Its great porches, polished colored concrete floors and open trusses in the great room along with the antiques and collectibles, give this bed and breakfast its unique ambiance. A wood-burning cookstove in the delightful country kitchen invites guests to a scrumptious homemade breakfast. Awake to the sounds of the desert birds and wildlife. The Desert Dove offers beautiful scenic mountain views, hiking and biking trails, horseback riding, and bird watching all nearby.

Desert Dove has two spacious guestrooms with a private entrance. Both rooms are beautifully decorated with antiques and collectibles. The Ross's have been collecting for twenty plus years. Their collection consists of antique toys, dolls, hats, quilts, graniteware, and pottery. They love their collections and wanted to

ABOVE: *THE DESERT DOVE AT SUNSET IS A MOST RELAXING RETREAT.*

share them with others. It had always been a dream of Harvey and Betty to open a bed and breakfast. When they found acreage near the Saguaro National Park East, they decided it was the place to build. Their son is an architect and designed the bed and breakfast for the couple, and they did the general contracting themselves. It was quite a learning experience for the Ross's, but their dream has come true.

The Watt Pottery was owned and operated by the Watt family. In July 1922, the Watt Pottery was incorporated in Crooksville, Ohio. Through the 1920s and early 1930s the Watt Pottery manufactured stoneware crocks, butter churns, preserve jars, and jugs. The Watt Pottery dropped its stoneware line in 1935. They chose instead to produce a more modern ovenware made of lightweight clay. This gave the kitchenware the necessary resilience to go from icebox to oven. In 1949, the Watt Pottery began hand decorating its wares with simple patterns found in nature using as few brush strokes as possible to allow low production costs. The hand-decorated patterns most sought after by today's collectors are Starflower, Apple, Cherry, Silhouette, Rooster, Dutch Tulip, American Red Bud (Tear Drop), Morning Glory, Autumn Foliage, Double Apple, and Tulip. The company remained in business until a fire halted production in 1965.

RIGHT: THE AREA ATOP KITCHEN CABINETS IS GREAT FOR DISPLAYING COLLECTIBLE POTTERY. TRY CREATING A PATTERN OR THEME SUCH AS ALTERNATING PLATES AND BOWLS OR ALL CROCKS. HERE BETTY GROUPS PITCHERS AND LARGE BOWLS.

INSET ABOVE: THINK ABOUT YOUR COLLECTIBLE. WATT POTTERY HAS MANY DESIGNS. HERE BETTY PAIRED HER APPLE PATTERN WITH OTHER APPLE PARAPHERNALIA INCLUDING SCALES, A CRATE AND A FRAMED APPLE PRINT. TRY IT WITH YOUR PARTICULAR TYPE OF POTTERY.

LEFT: SINCE WATT POTTERY WAS CREATED AND USED DURING THE EARLY PART OF THE 20TH CENTURY, HOOSIERS ARE NATURAL DISPLAY AREAS FOR THIS PARTICULAR POTTERY.

© Michael Carroll

The Notchland Inn

Hart's Location, New Hampshire

Ed Butler, Les Schoof and Kath Harris

Cobalt Glassware

ABOVE: THE NOTCHLAND INN BOASTS OF BEAUTIFUL VISTAS ESPECIALLY WHEN THE FLOWERS ARE IN FULL BLOOM.

This comfortable 1860s granite mansion is located on 100 acres in the midst of beautiful mountain vistas. The Notchland Inn rests atop a knoll at the base of Mount Bemis and looks out over Mounts Hope and Crawford. An operating inn since the 1920s, Notchland's traditions of hospitality are inextricably linked to Abel Crawford's 18th century Mt. Crawford House which stood on this property, and whose tavern is now the inn's dining room. Crawford Notch itself is a monument to his family name and to the history of The White Mountains.

The front parlor, designed by Gustav Stickley, a founder of the Arts and Crafts movement, is a perfect place to cozy up by the fire or to visit with other guests. Here, guests may try one of the board games or contribute to the perpetual "puzzle-in-progress." The music room draws guests to the piano or to the stereo to listen to music that they personally select. If daydreaming is top priority, the views of the inn property and mountains are wonderful from the sunroom. Finally, the Notchland's eclectic library is a great place to sip coffee and read a book.

Nature's wonders abound at Notchland. Guests enjoy activities that vary with the seasons including hiking, mountain biking, cross-country skiing, snowshoeing, fishing, swimming, or skating topped off with a soak in the wooden hot tub that sits in a gazebo by the pond. Outdoors, the ficus trees share space with blooming plants and a babbling fountain, not to mention the various wildlife. The Notchland Inn has 8,000 feet of Saco River frontage on the property. A brook cascades down Bemis Mountain and enters the Saco River just above the inn's granite gorge creating one of the area's best swimming holes. In addition to swimming, The Davis Path, which ascends Mount Crawford and links to other trails leading to the summit of Mount Washington, starts just across the road from the Inn. Many other hiking trails begin on and near Notchland.

After living in New York City for more than 10 years and renovating two 125-year old brownstones, Ed and Les began thinking of about "moving on" in the summer of 1990. At first, the search was nationwide but then narrowed to the Northeast, then New England, and finally to New Hampshire and Vermont. After three years of several close calls, they made one last trip to look at property. They knew they had found their next home with that first look. The unique property had just the right amount of warmth, grace, and elegance framed by an inspiring backdrop. Ed and Les were owners of Notchland just three months later. "From the outset of our search, we had said that the right property would 'sing' to us. From that first moment, Notchland sang a fine tune who's song grows richer and more enticing each day."

ABOVE: THIS IS A GOOD EXAMPLE OF VISUAL TEXTURE. THOUGH ALL THE PIECES ARE THE SAME COLOR, THE STYLE AND SHAPE OF THE PIECES MAKE THE DISPLAY INTERESTING.

BELOW: HERE ED AND LES DISPLAY VARIOUS COBALT PIECES ON THE MANTEL. THEY GROUPED SEVERAL PIECES ON EACH END OF THE MANTEL PAYING SPECIAL ATTENTION TO THE VISUAL TEXTURE OF THE ITEMS. THEN THEY PLACED AN INTRICATELY DESIGNED DISH IN THE CENTER BY ITSELF. THE LARGE PRINT IS SIMPLE AND INCORPORATES THE COBALT COLOR ALONG WITH LEMON YELLOW TO COMPLEMENT THE BLUE HUES.

Photo courtesy of Ronald J. Glassman.

Wedgwood Inn

New Hope, Pennsylvania

Carl and Nadine Glassman

Wedgwood China

Wedgwood Inn is one of three bed and breakfast properties owned by Carl and Nadine "Dinie" Glassman in the New Hope historic district. The 19th century home offers nine guestrooms and suites with a distinctive style. The Wedgwood Collection of Historic Inns has been offering bed and breakfast lodging since 1982. Carl and Dinie have renovated the three 19th-century homes on over two acres of landscaped grounds in New Hope's Historic District. The large guestrooms combine the period charm of hardwood floors, lofty windows, antique furnishings, and Wedgwood pottery with the modern conveniences guests come to expect in the 21st century. Although only a minute from the bustling artists' colony, the inn offers a pastoral respite with gazebos and picnic tables shaded by

ABOVE: WEDGWOOD INN IS A BLUE "PAINTED LADY" AND A VICTORIAN CHARMER.

century-old trees brightened by colorful flowers which border the expansive lawns.

A day at Wedgwood begins with a breakfast of fresh-squeezed orange juice, yogurt, granola, fresh fruit salad, home-baked muffins, breads, pastries, hot croissants, and just-made coffee and tea. Evenings wind down in conversation with other guests out in the gazebo or before the parlor fire and conclude in the comfort of a private room savoring the mint left on the pillow with a tiny glass of Carl's (secret recipe) almond liqueur.

A river community founded in 1681, New Hope is registered as a National Historic Site. Guests can absorb three centuries of architecture and history while leisurely exploring its historic sites, museums, covered bridges, art galleries, restaurants, flea markets, and numerous craft and antique shops. The inn's grounds were the site of a Revolutionary War encampment in December 1776, just prior to George Washington's famous crossing of the Delaware River.

Nadine and Carl Glassman had a dream to own a bed and breakfast country inn. They are part of a new class of professional who rejects suburban conformity and urban complexity. It was the life of the small town and gingerbread Victorian house filled with antiques that drew them. They have opened their inn to others who have the same dream and offer an opportunity to "apprentice" with them to see if the reality of owning an inn is as interesting as the fantasy.

Nadine and Carl have an extensive Wedgwood Pottery collection and use it as inspiration throughout the namesake bed and breakfast. Pieces are displayed on walls and high shelves that encircle rooms and are used in everyday dining. Nadine and Carl even used the distinctive Wedgwood colors to inspire the paint colors throughout the bed and breakfast.

Photo courtesy of Ronald J. Glassman.

RIGHT: YOU DON'T HAVE TO HAVE A MANTEL ON WHICH TO DISPLAY YOUR COLLECTIBLES. NADINE AND CARL USED VARIOUS TYPES OF MOLDING TO CREATE A HIGH SHELF THAT ENCIRCLES THE ROOM — A PERFECT DISPLAY AREA.

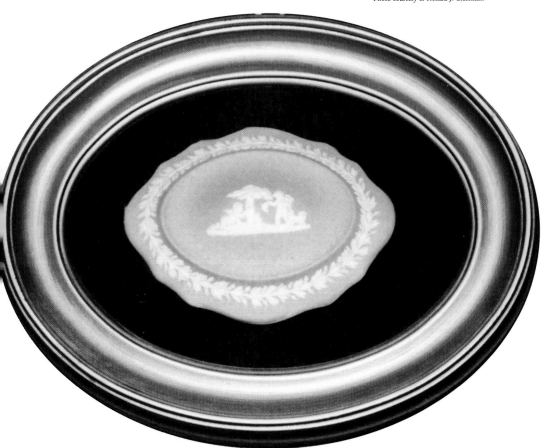

Photo courtesy of Ronald J. Glassman.

LEFT: THE GLASSMANS CAME UP WITH THIS UNIQUE IDEA FOR DISPLAYING AN ORPHANED LID. THEY SIMPLY POSITIONED THE LID ON A PIECE OF CLOTH AND FRAMED IT IN A COMPLEMENTARY GOLD LEAF FRAME.

LEFT: THIS HAND-PAINTED PLATTER SITS ON THE MANTEL.

BELOW: ONE OF JENEANE'S HAND-PAINTED TEACUPS WITH MATCHING SAUCER.

Stone Soup Inn

Indianapolis, Indiana
Jeneane Life

Hand-painted China

Located in the heart of the historic Old Northside, the Stone Soup Inn offers all the beauty and comfort of an upscale turn-of-the-century home. Decorated with a combination of Mission-style and Victorian-era antiques, guests will find a comfortable, convenient place to stay as they explore nearby historic sites and downtown attractions.

Jeneane ran a bed and breakfast on Nantucket Island during two of her college summers. That's how she fell in love with the industry. However, after graduating with a degree in Germanic Studies (German) and East Asian Languages and Literature (Japanese), Jeneane went to Japan to live for two years where she taught English.

Upon returning to Indiana, Jeneane took a job with an architectural engineering firm specializing in Japanese automotive clients. She worked there for ten years before choosing to have a baby and open her inn. Now Jeneane has 3 inns! She co-owns two of her inns with her parents. "I dragged them and my husband into the industry," she says. Jeneane just opened her newest endeavor in October 2001. It features very upscale guest rooms, an 80-seat gourmet restaurant and a full service day spa. "Innkeeping lets me be with my now 3-year-old son, which is very important to me," Jeneane points out.

Jeneane's collection of hand-painted china is more than just plates. She has plates, cups, saucers, sugar shakers, salt and pepper shakers, vanity trays, hot chocolate pots, candlesticks, etc. She uses her pieces to decorate her entry way and adjoining dining room.

"They are very interesting because everyday people painted them. Some are great and others look like someone needed glasses. What makes them so special is that most are signed by the ladies who created them. Some have dates, others have addresses, and some even have homemade logos. When jobs weren't readily available women would paint pieces and often sell them," Jeneane explains.

BELOW: THE STONE SOUP INN IS FORTUNATE TO HAVE SUCH A LOVELY BUILT-IN CHINA CABINET ALONG THE WALL OF ITS DINING ROOM. A PIECE OF MOLDING ALONG THE TOP MAKES A LEDGE PERFECT FOR DISPLAYING PLATES.

INSET: JUST ONE OF THE FINE PIECES OF HAND-PAINTED CHINA IN THE STONE SOUP COLLECTION.

LEFT: ONE WAY TO DISPLAY CHINA PLATES IS TO PUT THEM IN A PLATE RACK. PLATE RACKS COME IN VARIOUS SIZES AND STYLES AND CAN BE EASILY PURCHASED DEPENDING UPON YOUR PREFERENCES.

The Brickhouse Inn

Gettysburg, Pennsylvania
Craig and Marion Schmitz

Pharmacy Bottles

ABOVE: BUILT IN 1898 JUST AFTER THE CIVIL WAR, THE BRICKHOUSE INN IS LOCATED IN GETTYSBURG'S DOWNTOWN HISTORIC DISTRICT.

BELOW: MARION DISPLAYS PART OF HER COLLECTION OF ANTIQUE PHARMACY BOTTLES ATOP THIS ANTIQUE DESK.

Built in 1898 for a local banker, The Brickhouse Inn is located in Gettysburg's downtown historic district. This three story brick Victorian features a wrap around porch with rockers that invite guests to stop and relax a bit after a day of sightseeing and shopping. Family heirlooms and selected antiques give the gracious inn a warm atmosphere.

The search for a lifestyle change and a business to run together is what led Craig and Marion to their current profession as innkeepers. They spent two years researching, attending seminars, and looking at potential properties before deciding upon Gettysburg. Being a graduate of Gettysburg High School, Marion was familiar with the town itself. They happened upon the brick duplex shortly after it went on the market and

LEFT: *OF COURSE THE FIREPLACE MANTEL IS A GREAT PLACE FOR MORE COLORFUL BOTTLES.*

INSET: *THE HEARTH IS ALSO HOME TO SOME OF THE LARGER BOTTLES IN MARION'S COLLECTION.*

realized it was exactly what they were looking for all along. After ten months of renovations, the Schmitz's opened on July 4, 1996 with three guestrooms. An additional four rooms were opened May of 1997. Today, The Brickhouse Inn has ten guestrooms in two buildings. A full breakfast awaits guests each morning and is served in the dining room or outside on the garden patio during the summer months.

The Brickhouse Inn is home to a couple of collections. One is Marion's glass ball ornaments collection. Her collection began with pieces her parents had on their trees as children. She has added to the collection over the years by scouring antique shops including some ornaments from Germany and others of unknown origin. Another collection that Marion enjoys is her assortment of pharmacy bottles. As a pharmacist, Marion started her collection many years ago. What better way to enhance your career than to discover its history? Marion searches flea markets and antique stores for the bottles that now grace her parlor fireplace mantle. Her growing collection now includes bottles of varying color, size, and shapes.

Another Idea

You can enjoy your collection of bottles even if you don't have a mantel or piece of furniture on which to showcase them. Here bed and breakfast owner, Kathleen Janke of Gracehill created her own shelf on which to display her bottles. She created it out of a simple piece of crown molding that matches her trim. She hung this particular shelf over a doorway.

LEFT: THE STATELY CHARLEY MONTANA BED AND BREAKFAST WAS BUILT IN 1906 AND WAS A COMFORTABLE FAMILY HOME OF A MERE 8,000 SQUARE FEET!

INSET: PIECES OF JIM AND KATHERINE LEE'S FIRE KING COLLECTION.

Charley Montana Bed and Breakfast

Glendive, Montana

Jim and Katherine Lee

Fire King Dishes

Built in 1906 by railroader, rancher, banker Charles Krug, the Krug Mansion is now the site of Charley Montana Bed and Breakfast. This comfortable family home of 8,000 square feet has been on the National Register of Historic Places since 1976. Irene, the last surviving child of Charles and Annie Krug, was still living in the house until 1995. The house has an imposing brick edifice, but the view from the front entry is magic. The nine-foot-wide hall is an impressive entrance—quality without pretense. Ionic columns shield the stairway. Ceilings loom high above. Wood pocket doors are huge slabs of quarter-sawn oak. The woodwork reveals its original condition—gleaming with the depth created by ninety years of hand rubbing with oil. The leaded glass windows are tasteful and perfect. The rooms are large. Jim and Katherine Lee welcome visitors to the spacious accommodations.

Jim and Katherine have been asked why they chose to become bed and breakfast owners many, many times. They are city folks from Minnesota now living in Glendive, a small town in Montana. Jim retired from a 30-year career with Federal Cartridge Company, and Katherine is a retired attorney. Both love old houses and have updated and revamped other homes over time. Unlike some innkeepers, becoming bed and breakfast owners was not a dream Jim and Katherine carried through the years. In 1995, Jim and Katherine read about a canoe trip on the Upper Missouri in Montana. The article promised a week in primitive conditions, under the vast sky, in lands incredibly rugged and imposing. They made the trip, and were enchanted. While there, they picked up a land magazine curious about local land prices. A classic brick mansion in Glendive was among the properties listed. The eastern Montana home was huge, stunning, and unique. Curious about the house, Jim and Katherine drove south to Glendive.

After viewing the Krug Mansion, Jim and Katherine drove home with their heads crammed with thoughts of the remarkable Krug house. The house needed to be saved, and its quality deserved preservation. During the 9-hour car ride home, they explored what could be done with the building. It had been on the market for fifteen years, and was in the names of multiple Krug heirs who had been unable to cooperate sufficiently to consummate a sale in the past. The building was of a size and configuration to house retail shops, offices, or apartments. However, any conversion would damage its remarkable authenticity. Perhaps a bed and breakfast—eleven bedrooms, loads of common space. It took months to decide to buy the building, then months longer to obtain a mortgage for the unconventional property in the small Montana town. Then came the rehab, with weeks digging out the basement floor, and all the plumbing and wiring that go into updating an old house. Jim insisted on a manly name including Montana—hence Charley Montana, for Charles Krug and Jim's Montana grandfather, Charles Nelson.

Jim and Katherine's Fire King collection began in the late 1980s when Jim was starting over. His mother gifted him two Fire King mugs, which were then the only dishes he had to his name. Katherine was starting over at the same time, and had only a few dishes of her own. With that start, they began to seek out the lovely glass dishes in antique shops in Minnesota, and collected many at Depression Glass shows in Minneapolis. They now have more than 300 Fire King pieces. Most are in Jadeite green; others are blue, white, ivory, peach luster, and gray luster. The green dishes are often used by guests, and make a beautiful table on their own. They also combine beautifully with Jim and Katherine's other dish collections, which include Red Wing and pastel ring petalware. The shapes vary from the masculine restaurant ware to the dainty Jane Ray and Alice designs.

ABOVE: THE LARGE FIREPLACE AND MANTEL IS AN ATTRACTIVE BACKDROP FOR THE JADEITE BOWL AND PLATES. THE FIREPLACE SCREEN IS CREATED USING A TEXTILE THAT COMPLEMENTS THE COLOR OF THE JADEITE.

INSET: JUST A FEW OF THE LEE'S 300 PLUS PIECES OF JADEITE FIRE KING MUGS DISPLAYED ON A SHORT SHELF BETWEEN THE FIREPLACE AND THE DOORWAY.

B&B at Taylor's Corner

Woodstock, Connecticut
Doug and Peggy Tracy

Danish Porcelain

ABOVE: THE B&B AT TAYLOR'S CORNER IS DRESSED FOR THE HOLIDAYS WITH SIMPLE EVERGREEN WREATHS ADORNED WITH BRIGHT RED BOWS.

Located just three miles off Scenic Route 169 and nestled on a bend of a winding country road, the B&B at Taylor's Corner is an 18th century home listed on the National Register of Historic Places. The B&B at Taylor's Corner offers traditional lodging and even hearthside cooking in the romance of a completely restored 18th century, central chimney Colonial featuring eight fireplaces, two beehive ovens, wide-board floors and other architectural features common to the 18th century. The now antique "Connecticut Cottage" was moved here and attached to the east side of the original structure during the early 1800s.

During the 1700s, the five acres presently known as Taylor's Corner were part of the 500-acre "Allen Farm." It is believed that the road passed to the south of the house in that era, but it has since been relocated, leaving the house situated on a curve. Nell Taylor operated a private boarding school during the early 1900s, thus establishing the property's present name. It has also served as a popular biker's hostel and an herbary.

Guests are invited to relax in a spacious guestroom overlooking herb gardens, with fields in the distance or by one of the cozy fireplaces for winter nights. Take a nature hike along a country dirt road just across the street; do some seasonal apple, pumpkin or berry picking at one of the local orchards or be real adventurous and go hot air ballooning.

Each morning brings with it the aroma of coffee brewing and muffins baking. When Peggy offers a traditional hearth-cooked meal, she means real, early American, hearth-cooked cuisine. The B&B at Taylor's Corner welcomes guests who admire the beauty and craftsmanship of colonial times, as well as the rural atmosphere, creaking floors, crooked walls and traditional cooking that complement the hospitality of an older home.

Guests at B&B at Taylor's Corner are within seconds of some wonderful antiquing, the casinos, Mystic Seaport and Old Sturbridge Village. For those who are looking for more athletic adventures there are four nearby state parks where they can go hiking or swimming. Golf courses and tennis courts are nearby as well.

ABOVE: THE BLUE AND WHITE SCENES OF THESE PORCELAIN PLATES ARE ELEGANTLY AND SIMPLY DISPLAYED ALONG SIDE THE REGULATOR CLOCK.

LEFT: THE GLASS DOORS OF THE HUTCH ALLOW THESE PORCELAIN PIECES TO BE SEEN WITHOUT BEING AT RISK OF HANDLING BY THE INN'S NUMEROUS GUESTS. ANOTHER VERTICAL DISPLAY OF PLATES CAN BE SEEN ALONG THE RIGHT SIDE OF THE HUTCH.

Whispering Pines
High Falls, New York
Celia and HD Seupel

Pottery

CELIA SEUPEL WELCOMES GUESTS TO THE WHISPERING PINES BED AND BREAKFAST.

Whispering Pines is a contemporary, cozy chalet surrounded by 50 acres of private woods on all sides. A cathedral ceiling, skylights, innumerable windows, and an interior balcony between the two upstairs bedrooms create a spacious, light-filled atmosphere. The fireplace is kept ablaze from fall to spring, and all summer, the woodland breezes wander the house through open windows and doors.

Celia and HD fell in love with their home before they ever thought about opening a bed and breakfast. What first captivated them was the forest surrounding the house on all sides — 50 acres of rustling trees populated only by the wild deer, turkey, and great horned owls. Second was the house itself. The living room's cathedral, knotty pine ceiling, the skylights, and the sliding glass doors that open to the woods — not to mention the Jacuzzis and a bedroom floor made of pure cherry — captivated the couple.

Inveterate entrepreneurs, at first Celia and HD thought they might build vacation cabins on the property, but as they moved in and got comfortable, they realized that the house itself was perfectly suited for an inn. The more they investigated, the more this idea made sense. When Celia and HD moved to High Falls in New York's Hudson Valley, they had no idea that they were settling into a very special vacation spot — they just loved their new home. But with so many fabulous attractions nearby, Celia and HD had lucked upon a great location. The Shawangunk Mountains — famed far and wide for rock-climbing — as well as Mohonk Preserve and Minnewaska State Park were just fifteen minutes from the house, not to mention the Antiques Trail and the Wineries Trail. Celia and HD plunged into the bed and breakfast business with both feet. That was six years ago, and they're still having fun.

Celia never started out to collect anything, but she's a pushover for traditions. Her mom always collected wonderful handcrafted pottery, and she gave Celia her first few pieces. In fact, when Celia was a child, the two of them took pottery classes together. Now both ladies have great collections! There are many local artisans in the High Falls area. In fact, the "Pottery Trail" runs right through High Falls. Celia also collects imported pottery from Japan. "I am particularly attracted to colorful and unusual glazes. I also love pieces that have unusual shapes and pieces that are not thrown on the wheel, that really show the potter's hand," she confesses. "Pottery is not only beautiful to the eye, it is wonderful to touch and use. It's as much a tactile delight to sip tea from a warm blue-glazed mug, as it is a visual and gustatory pleasure. While I might use a piece like a vase or potpourri dish in a room, I consider our huge breakfast buffet and afternoon tea pottery display one of the highlights of my decorating. In my opinion, your setting for breakfast sounds as much of a keynote for your inn as does your bedding and the pictures on the walls," explains Celia. She goes on to say, "Whispering

Pines is a contemporary home, filled with natural wood, windows, and light. Everything I do features a relaxed, comfortable atmosphere and natural beauty. While delicate china might fit into an historic inn filled with antiques, our pottery really reflects our inn – sturdy and lovely, full of color and light, reflecting the simple beauty of nature."

INSET ABOVE: DON'T BE AFRAID TO MIX AND MATCH. AS LONG AS PIECES HAVE COMPLEMENTARY COLORS AND PATTERNS, PLACE SETTINGS DON'T HAVE TO BE MADE UP OF MATCHING PIECES.

ABOVE: CELIA COLLECTS POTTERY FROM VARIOUS ARTISTS. HER TABLE IS SET EACH DAY WITH PLACE SETTINGS OF VARIOUS STYLES AND PIECES.

LEFT: THE STURDY POTTERY PIECES THAT CELIA COLLECTS ARE PERFECT FOR SERVING GUESTS IN FRONT OF A BLAZING FIRE.

Toys

Dolls
Teddy Bears

Cameo Rose
Victorian
Country Inn

Belleville, Wisconsin

Gary and Dawn Bahr

Dolls

The Cameo Rose Victorian Country Inn is a romantic Victorian-style bed and breakfast getaway located in the Madison, Wisconsin area. It sits on 120 acres of hills, woods, views, and trails midway between Madison and New Glarus, Wisconsin (America's Little Switzerland). There guests enjoy elegant and comfortable lodging accommodations, old-fashioned hospitality, immense peace and quiet, or a hand-in-hand stroll on miles of private hiking trails. The gateway to beautiful southern Wisconsin, the Cameo Rose is situated near several state parks and bike trails and the University of Wisconsin.

ABOVE LEFT: THIS NEWLY CONSTRUCTED VICTORIAN IS A ROMANTIC GETAWAY AT CHRISTMAS WITH THE BLANKET OF SNOW AND THE BEDECKED WRAP-AROUND PORCH.

INSET: DOLLS LEND THEMSELVES TO DISPLAYS SUCH AS THIS ONE IN WHICH THE TWO YOUNG LADIES ARE HAVING TEA. FINDING MINIATURE ACCESSORIES TO ACCOMPANY DOLLS IN SUCH SCENES CAN BE VERY ENJOYABLE IN AND OF ITSELF.

Like so many other proprietors in the business, Dawn had dreamed of owning her own bed and breakfast. After more than 20 years in business administration, she decided to do something more creative with her life. Dawn and Gary's search for the perfect bed and breakfast began with the "Home of the Week" section in the Sunday paper where a lovely reproduction Victorian was featured. Reluctant to move to the city in order to start their tourist-centered business, Dawn and Gary chose to build a "new" Victorian mansion right on Gary's 120-acre family farm. Once the house was built, Dawn began pursuing the creative passions in her life—one of them being doll making.

Dawn devoted three hours per week to her class on doll making over the course of several years. There Dawn learned to make her very own dolls including the sculpting, carving out of the eyes, mouth and hands, firing and painting. She created cloth bodies for her dolls and stuffed and attached them to the porcelain head and appendages. Each of Dawn's dolls is unique utilizing vintage fabrics and jewelry, customized for the season in which it is displayed in the bed and breakfast. Each bears her initials and date of creation at the base of the head so that she may pass the collection onto her daughter Jennifer. But for now, the dolls enjoy their own private parties amongst the guests at the inn.

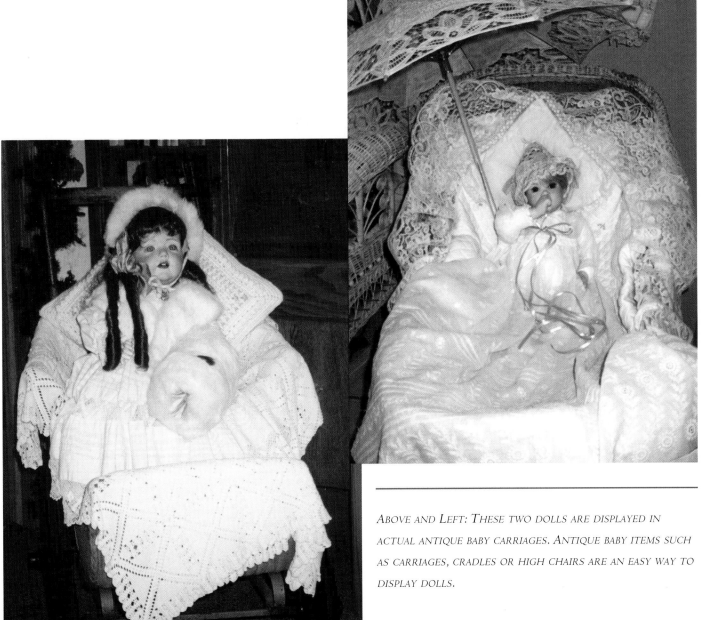

ABOVE AND LEFT: THESE TWO DOLLS ARE DISPLAYED IN ACTUAL ANTIQUE BABY CARRIAGES. ANTIQUE BABY ITEMS SUCH AS CARRIAGES, CRADLES OR HIGH CHAIRS ARE AN EASY WAY TO DISPLAY DOLLS.

Country Life Bed and Breakfast

Greenwich, New York
Richard and Wendy Duvall

Teddy Bears

ABOVE: THE SWEEPING MOUNTAIN VIEWS ARE JUST ONE OF COUNTRY LIFE BED AND BREAKFAST'S ASSETS.

Begun on Long Island in 1982, Country Life Bed and Breakfast is nestled in the rolling hills of Washington County, New York, near Saratoga Springs. One of the largest farm areas in the United States, it is located just a short distance from Vermont's best ski areas and the Adirondack Mountains. The unending dramas of the changing seasons, the sweeping mountain views, the climactic sunsets, the natural wonders... all these assets made it easy for Richard and Wendy to choose this 118-acre farm to be their second edition of Country Life Bed and Breakfast.

Country Life Bed and Breakfast has hosted hundreds of wonderful guests from all over the USA, Canada and abroad. Guests can settle in and enjoy the most glorious sunsets east of the Grand Canyon while they unwind by the fireplace with a cup of hot cocoa or wintertime skiing is just 15 minutes away. In the morning, they can enjoy an ample and varied breakfast with a leisurely cup of coffee on the deck of Richard and Wendy's Saratoga bed and breakfast. For those interested in a more leisurely visit, guests can stroll around the pastures or through the pine woods alongside the brook, take a ride with Richard and Wendy in one of their antique autos, then set out on their own for a day of sightseeing. Those guests who like a more invigorating outing can play in the natural swimming hole with two waterfalls and a rockslide. An old mill stream runs through the center of the farm at the Saratoga bed and breakfast. The foundation of stone for the old mill has remained alongside the stream for more than 200 years. A bridge across the stream leads to 30 acres of old woodlands filled with trails and wildlife, perfect for hiking.

Richard and Wendy have two collections that they enjoy. One is a collection of cut crystal. Wendy displays this collection on side tables, buffets, and on built in bookshelves. Richard and Wendy also have a small collection of teddy bears that spend their evening with guests in their rooms. The bears can be found on the beds, on benches, and in an antique cradle.

ABOVE: TEDDY BEARS, LIKE DOLLS, HAVE A HUMAN QUALITY ABOUT THEM THAT MAKE THEM EASY TO DISPLAY USING ITEMS SUCH AS THIS BENCH ACCOMPANIED HERE BY A TEDDY BEAR BOOK.

LEFT: BECAUSE TEDDY BEARS ARE SO HUMAN IN NATURE, BABY ITEMS SUCH AS CRADLES AND HIGH CHAIRS CAN HELP CREATE HEARTWARMING DISPLAYS. HERE, INNKEEPER WENDY DUVALL DISPLAYS AN ANTIQUE CHILD'S DRESS WITH HER CRADLE FULL OF BEARS.

The Dolls' House

Annapolis, Maryland

John and Barbara Dugan

Dolls

The Dolls' House is a late Victorian shingle-style home located in the heart of the historic district of Annapolis, Maryland just one block from the City Dock and Market Square. A one-minute walk will take you to charming shops, restaurants or an evening of great music. A five-minute walk will take you to the State Capitol, other historic sites and, of course, the Naval Academy

The Dolls' House was originally built for a Maryland judge in 1901. The genteel taste of the Victorian period can be easily seen in the tiger oak woodwork, Georgia pine floors, brass and tile fireplaces,

high ceilings, large windows and marble vestibule. All convey a welcoming taste of past and present amenities. The Dugans decorated The Dolls' House in a sort of "Victorian Whimsy" style with furniture and decor true to that nostalgic time. Open the front gate, climb the porch steps, and enter a delightful family home decorated with antiques throughout, including the owners' private doll collection.

ABOVE: AS ITS NAME SUGGESTS, THE DOLLS' HOUSE BED AND BREAKFAST IS HOME OF BARBARA DUGAN'S VAST DOLL COLLECTION.

LEFT: THIS ANTIQUE DOLL SITS IN A VICTORIAN WICKER CHAIR WITH BLUE UPHOLSTERED CUSHIONS THAT ACCENT HER LOVELY VICTORIAN GARB.

Guests are invited to enjoy a hearty breakfast in the dining room or on the sun deck. They may whittle away the day on the front porch swing or in the rear flower garden or arrange an eventful day visiting the nearby attractions of Annapolis.

The Dolls' House obviously got its name from the vast collection of antique dolls that the owners have displayed throughout the bed and breakfast. Guests can of course, find dolls in display cases, but they can also find dolls enjoying their bed while they have gone out for the day, in an antique cradle, or other various places. The Dugans are collectors at heart. In addition to their doll collection, they also have an eclectic collection of Victorian furniture, dolls' house miniatures, and various antique glassware and wood carvings.

The Dugans settled on a turn-of-the-century transitional Victorian Arts and Crafts home in Annapolis about 7 years ago. It was constructed in 1901 and is believed to be the newest house on the street. "We could not have found a lovelier place. The neighborhood reminds us so much of our previous home in London, England."

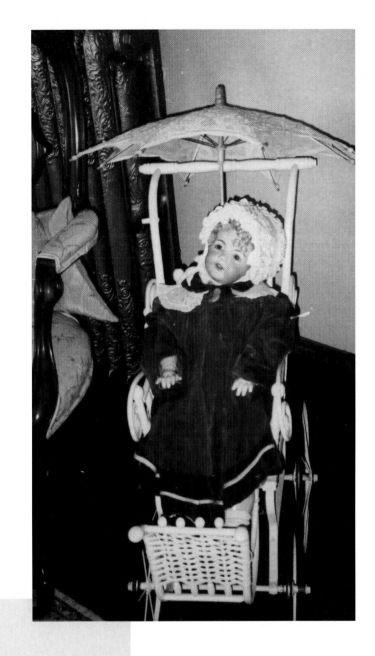

ABOVE: THIS ANTIQUE PORCELAIN DOLL FITS PERFECTLY INTO THE CHILD'S WICKER BABY CARRIAGE WITH ATTACHED PARASOL.

LEFT: THIS ANTIQUE CRADLE IS HOME TO SEVERAL OF BARBARA'S PORCELAIN AND COMPOSITION BABY DOLLS.

Rosewood Country Inn

Bradford, New Hampshire

Dick and Lesley Marquis

Teddy Bears

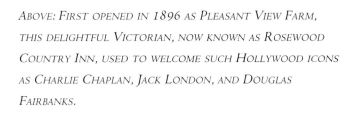

Surrounded by 12 acres of grounds and award winning gardens, The Rosewood Country Inn is located in the delightful town of Bradford, New Hampshire— just 90 miles from Boston. The bordering stone walls conjure up images of its Early American tradition, and the sunlit porches and common rooms are inviting with country elegance, warmth, and relaxation.

Built in 1850, Mr. and Mrs. Edward Messer first opened their inn as Pleasant View Farm in 1896. Rates back then were a mere $5.00-$7.00 a week but references were required. It became a well-known resort and the guest list has included such Hollywood icons as Mr. & Mrs. Charlie Chaplan, Jack London, Gloria Swanson, Mary Pickford, Douglas Fairbanks, and the Gish Sisters. The Messer Family continued to operate the inn until 1956.

ABOVE: FIRST OPENED IN 1896 AS PLEASANT VIEW FARM, THIS DELIGHTFUL VICTORIAN, NOW KNOWN AS ROSEWOOD COUNTRY INN, USED TO WELCOME SUCH HOLLYWOOD ICONS AS CHARLIE CHAPLAN, JACK LONDON, AND DOUGLAS FAIRBANKS.

INSET: THIS TEDDY SITS IN A BARN RED CHILD'S CHAIR IN FRONT OF A STENCILED MURAL ON THE WALL.

In 1991, Dick and Lesley Marquis purchased the inn after years of abandonment. It was gutted and filled with debris, but the Marquis' could easily see the property's potential. After a drastic renovation, the country Victorian inn now has 11 guestrooms and suites offering cozy fireplaces and Jacuzzis.

Lesley and Dick entered the world of innkeeping after years in the medical field. Both wanted a slower paced life and country atmosphere in which to raise their two daughters, Becki and Sarah. Rhode Island natives, Dick enjoys hunting and fishing, and Lesley likes to spend time gardening and cooking. They even published two cookbooks entitled, *Brunch at the Rosewood Country Inn* and *Christmas Traditions*.

Lesley began her teddy bear collection about 20 years ago when her children gave her bears for Christmas. Her collection of teddy bears grew over the year along with her daughters. Several bears now reside at the inn to be enjoyed by family and guests alike. Now guests send bears as "thank you's" in return for their enjoyable weekend.

ABOVE: THESE LADIES ARE ENJOYING TEA TOGETHER. BEARS CAN EASILY BE DISPLAYED IN SCENES JUST LIKE DOLLS. THIS SCENE USES A SAMPLER OF COMPLEMENTARY COLORS AS A BACKDROP.

BELOW: GUESTS WILL HAVE TO FIND SOMEWHERE ELSE TO SIT IF THEY WANT TO BE NEAR THE SMOLDERING FIRE AS THIS BARN RED BENCH IS TAKEN BY LESLEY'S FAVORITE BEARS.

Watercolor courtesy of Lindsey Truby.

Chez Amis

Annapolis, Maryland

Don and Mickie Deline

Teddy Bears

ABOVE: CHEZ AMIS OR "HOUSE OF FRIENDS" IS AN APPROPRIATELY NAMED BED AND BREAKFAST THAT WAS ONCE THREE SEPARATE BUILDINGS.

A former corner grocery owned by the Sams Brothers, Chez Amis is comprised of three separate buildings. Two former row houses were built as single family dwellings in 1885-1891 and a third corner building was built in 1903 that made-up the single-story store. In 1920, the three buildings were merged to create Sams Brothers Grocery Store on the first floor and a residence for George Sams on the second. The store was converted into a bed and breakfast in 1987.

Proprietors Don and Mickie Deline purchased the bed and breakfast in 1994 after much thought and prayer. "Ok, God, you know how stupid we are. . .if we are supposed to move to Annapolis, let us both love the same thing, otherwise we will know we are not supposed to move. PS. . .Don't be subtle, we are not smart enough to figure it out!" After 25 years as a JAG officer and living in 17 different places worldwide, Don

and his wife, Mickie, fell in love with and purchased the oddly shaped building. They originally just wanted to buy a home in the Annapolis area, not a business, but nothing else was available that they both liked. From the strangely shaped rooms, to the light airy feeling of the main living area, to the great location, they loved everything about the bed and breakfast that was named Chez Amis, "House of Friends."

Chez Amis is best described as cozy, quaint, charming and comfortable. Each room has collections that represent Don and Mickie's 36 years together. Mickie didn't realize that she was a collector until she organized the family furnishings for the living areas and four guestrooms. She collects quilts, teapots, bears and bunnies, Santas, chess sets, and beer steins. Mickie's bear collection began years ago, and they are everywhere. She says she only buys them when they "talk" to her, and they look her right in the eye. "Only another bear collector can relate," she says. Her favorite is Barnaby, a bear purchased in a German toy factory in 1974 for their then four-year-old daughter, Michele. Mickie officially adopted Barnaby for her 50th birthday.

Photograph courtesy Ron Craig.

ABOVE: THE GERMAN POTATO WAGON FILLED
WITH BEARS AND BUNNIES GREET GUESTS AS
THEY ARRIVE FOR A FULL GOURMET
BREAKFAST.

LEFT: THIS APPLE LADDER FROM GERMANY
WAS RETRIEVED FROM THE TRASH. IT IS
INTERESTING IN AND OF ITSELF, BUT IT ALSO
MAKES UNIQUE SHELVING FOR BEARS OF
ASSORTED SIZES.

Photograph courtesy Ron Craig.

Mill Creek Homestead

Bird in Hand, Pennsylvania

Frank and Vicki Alfone

Dolls

ABOVE: THIS 18TH CENTURY STONE HOUSE IN LANCASTER COUNTY, PENNSYLVANIA, IS SITUATED IN A SMALL VILLAGE IN THE HEART OF PENNSYLVANIA DUTCH COUNTRY.

Joseph Steer was one of four Quakers warranted surveys at Bird in Hand on January 19, 1733 by John and Thomas Penn, sons of William Penn. An innkeeper, Joseph owned the Red Lion Inn and the Bird in Hand Inn. He built his first log house in the mid to late 1700s and later replaced it with a more substantial stone house. Over the years, the structure has been home to more than 15 families and was one of about 30 stops on the Underground Railroad. The house remained a family home until 1993 when Frank and Vicki established Mill Creek Homestead Bed and Breakfast. Though the house has undergone many restorative changes, the post and beam construction and the 2-foot thick walls are still a marvel.

When looking for property to establish their bed and breakfast, Frank and Vicki wanted something that was small enough for them to give guests the personalized service and pampering that they felt guests expected and deserved from a bed and breakfast. They found the 18th century stone home in the heart of Pennsylvania Dutch country and felt that the location was ideal. The layout of the house was perfect for four guestrooms on the second floor, and Frank and Vicki converted the third floor to living quarters for themselves. There was also an inground heated pool on the property with gardens and landscaping that is a rare amenity for a bed and breakfast.

ABOVE: VICKI USES AN ANTIQUE WOODEN HIGH CHAIR TO SEAT HER DOLL APPROPRIATELY DRESSED IN AMISH CLOTHING.

Because there was little information on how to start a bed and breakfast at that time, Vicki began by making phone calls to determine what was required to begin a bed and breakfast. From there, the Alfones added bathrooms and central air. Frank, an electrician with many years of construction experience, is the inn's maintenance man, which is critical to the inn's operation. Vicki is a nurse and feels that it is just natural for her to nurture.

The inn is furnished with family heirlooms and pieces that the Alfones purchased at estate sales and antique shops. Dolls are a particular favorite at the homestead including Frank and Vicki's daughter, Nicole's collection of American Girl Dolls. Dolls can be found throughout the home, and at Christmas dolls are incorporated in the decorating or can be found sitting under the tree.

Another Idea

Dolls can be especially interesting collectibles to display because they are so human. Not only can you use real infant items such as high chairs and cradles to display dolls, but it is quite easy to create a setting almost like a scene from a play. Here, Gary and Dawn Bahr of Cameo Rose have created one doll's wedding day complete with stained glass window and flowers.

Textiles

Beadwork
Clothing
Purses
Quilts
Samplers
Tablecloths
Wedding Dresses

The Red Barn Bed and Breakfast

Jamesport, New York

Linda and Jim Slezak

Quilts

The Red Barn Bed and Breakfast offers three guest bedrooms, one of which is a family suite in a lovingly restored 1877 farm house once owned by Lemuel Beecher Hallock, grandson of one of the originating farm families on the North Fork. The Red Barn acreage has some of the original outbuildings and one of the most picturesque barns in the area. Relaxing in a hammock under a shady maple tree, sipping lemonade in a rocking chair on the porch, a friendly game of horseshoes or croquet on the lawn, bird watching, stargazing, this is what the Red Barn Bed and Breakfast is all about!

Proprietors Linda and Jim Slezak sought a bed and breakfast on Long Island because they always felt that Long Island had so much to offer especially the North

ABOVE: A PICTURESQUE VIEW OF THE RED BARN THAT GIVES THE RED BARN BED AND BREAKFAST ITS NAME.

INSET: THE WRAP-AROUND PORCH IS JUST ONE OF THE INVITING PLACES TO "SIT A SPELL" AT THE RED BARN BED AND BREAKFAST.

Fork. When they saw this property, they said, "It just felt right." Largely unspoiled, the North Fork has huge tracks of farmland, beautiful beaches, wineries and farm stands all within one and a half hours drive of New York City. Jim is also an amateur astronomer so to him, the best feature of this area is the dark night sky with conditions good enough to see the Milky Way with the naked eye.

The guest bedrooms are comfortable and pleasingly decorated — many with Linda's quilts. Linda has a sizable quilt collection that she loves to use and display throughout the bed and breakfast. "I love quilts because they are so colorful and graphic." You can find many of Linda's charming old quilts on the beds, but she also uses them as wall art. She hangs her quilts using special quilt holders that are easily found or just by using simple curtain rods attached to the wall. "To me, nothing looks better on a bed or on a wall than a charming old quilt," says Linda.

RIGHT: ONE WAY THAT LINDA SLEZAK DISPLAYS HER ANTIQUE QUILTS IS FROM A SIMPLE BRASS CURTAIN ROD ATTACHED TO THE WALL OF ONE OF THE GUESTROOMS.

BELOW: QUILTS CAN BE FUNCTIONAL AND DECORATIVE. HERE LINDA DISPLAYS EXAMPLES OF HER QUILT COLLECTION ON BOTH THE BED AND THE WALL USING ONE OF THE MANY QUILT HANGERS AVAILABLE ON THE MARKET DESIGNED SO THAT THEY DON'T DAMAGE THE FABRIC.

The Old Brick Inn

St. Michaels, Maryland
Martha Strickland
Vintage Tablecloths

ABOVE: THE MAIN HOUSE OF THE OLD BRICK INN IS A BRICK FEDERAL STYLE BUILDING CONSTRUCTED AS A PRIVATE RESIDENCE IN 1816.

INSET: INNKEEPER MARTHA STRICKLAND USES VINTAGE TABLECLOTHS IN HER DINING AREA WHERE GUESTS CAN ENJOY THEM.

Listed on the National Register of Historic Places, the Old Brick Inn is comprised of two newly restored buildings. The main house, facing Talbot Street, was originally called the Old Inn, and dates back to 1816. Shipwright Wrightson Jones constructed the wonderful Federal style building as a private residence. In 1985, a former owner constructed the current carriage house building on the site of the original "carriage house." Over the years, the beautiful buildings have housed an assortment of businesses including a pharmacy, a Masonic lodge, a bank, a real estate office, an apartment building, and most recently, a private residence and antique gallery.

Located in the heart of St. Michael's, The Old Brick Inn is just an hour and a half drive from the Washington-Baltimore metropolitan area, and a 45-minute drive to Annapolis. Guests are sure to find something do in "the town that fooled the British." The Chesapeake Bay Maritime Museum, wonderful gift shops, galleries, antique shops and restaurants are just a short walk from the front door. Maryland's beautiful Eastern Shore is the perfect place to take long bike rides. When guests return, they are welcome to take a dip in the in-ground pool, relax in the private New Orleans-style courtyard, or unwind in the beautiful garden.

LEFT: VINTAGE TABLECLOTHS HAVE RECENTLY SEEN AN INCREASE IN INTEREST AND PRICE BECAUSE OF BEING FEATURED ON VARIOUS HOME SHOWS. THEREFORE, THEY ARE BECOMING MUCH MORE DIFFICULT TO FIND.

The Historic Old Brick Inn is a magical place, where guests can relax and unwind. The Main House, circa 1816, and Carriage House, circa 1985, feature twelve luxurious rooms, individually decorated, in an eclectic style. Some are traditional in flavor, and some are very unique, with distinct themes, such as the Guinevere and Annie Oakley Suites. The Honeymoon Suite features a beautiful formal living room area with fireplace, and a marble-floored bedroom and bath with whirlpool tub and shower.

Weather permitting, guests may eat a lavish continental breakfast outside in the private, New Orleans-style brick courtyard. Otherwise it is served in the cheerful dining room where most of Martha's collection resides, of course. Guests love to reminisce about the tablecloths that their mothers used to use and compare them to Martha's. But as Martha Strickland points out, these vintage tablecloths are becoming much more popular and difficult to find after being featured on various home shows including one hosted by another lady named Martha. Therefore, these vintage tablecloths are becoming more expensive as well.

Another Idea

You enjoy vintage tablecloths, but the pieces you have aren't in a suitable condition to use on the table? Try creating a valance or swag with them. You can enjoy the look while you hide some of the flaws.

Gracehill

Townsend, Tennessee

Kathleen Janke

Purses

ABOVE: A NEWLY CONSTRUCTED BED AND BREAKFAST, GRACEHILL OFFERS GUESTS A STUNNING VIEW OF THE SMOKY MOUNTAIN NATIONAL PARK.

Gracehill was several years in the making. Owner/Innkeeper Kathleen Janke had a vision of building an exceptional home on a mountain with a great view. Her first challenge was finding the right piece of property. She hiked the hills and pieces of property for sale for two years before eventually finding the 10 acres on which she would locate her home. The building site was cleared, and she ended up with a 360-degree view and a breathtaking backdrop for her special home that neighbors the Great Smoky Mountain National Park.

The project not only included building a home from the ground up but also building a road to a remote spot on top of a mountain. Prior to this project, Kathy's background had been in police communications, landscaping, and, along with her mother Marilyn, owned both a campground/cabin rental, and a restaurant/catering business. After they sold this business, Kathy

wanted to understand as much of the building process as possible. Therefore, during the two years of scouting for property, she went to work part time for the construction company she thought she would choose to build her home.

Almost five years in the making, it is apparent to all who visit that this home is meant to be shared with others. Whether by soaking in the whirlpool tub, enjoying the spectacular views, sitting on the veranda reading a book, enjoying a romantic gourmet meal, or just sharing some private time with a soul mate, guests at Gracehill enjoy a decadence rarely experienced as they revitalize themselves.

Gracehill, like most homes, has become a backdrop to Kathy's various collections. These include old bottles, carved wooden spoons, antique badges and locks and keys. Kathy also has a stunning collection of vintage beaded purses. They feature many unique designs. She had lighted built-ins created on either side of her fireplace in her master bedroom to display the purses.

Another Idea

A glass-topped coffee table would be a wonderful way to display pieces such as Kathleen's purses. Here Penny Rembe of Los Poblanos Inn displays her beaded purses.

ABOVE: KATHY'S MASTER SUITE INCLUDES LIGHTED BUILT-INS ON EITHER SIDE OF HER FIREPLACE SPECIFICALLY DESIGNED TO DISPLAY HER PURSE COLLECTION.

INSET: KATHY'S COLLECTION FEATURES INTRICATELY BEADED PURSES OF ALL SHAPES AND SIZES.

Gwendolyn's Inn
Perkinsville, Vermont
Laurie Hathaway

Vintage Clothing

Gwendolyn's Inn is an 1872 Victorian gambrel mansard mansion located on the historic Main Street in the charming village of Perkinsville, Vermont. Once known as the Old Call Mansion according to the deed, the period Victorian has all the amenities one would expect – dramatic curved foyer and staircase, original oak and mahogany raised panels, original claw-foot tubs, and hand-painted murals. Many guests liken the inn to a museum with the exception that they can touch the antiques. "I find the ingenuity of the Victorian craftspeople fascinating," Laurie explains. "Antiques usually have a practical purpose along with the pleasure in their beauty."

ABOVE: GWENDOLYN'S INN IS A COLORFUL MANSARD MANSION THAT BRINGS LIFE TO EVEN THE DREARIEST VERMONT WINTERS.

The restored mansion is surrounded by formal English gardens including Laurie's exquisite hollyhocks, a necessity for any English garden. Guests are invited to sit on the veranda and simply enjoy the myriad of colors and the enveloping scents. The hammock is the perfect place to listen to the soothing sound of the waterfalls across the street.

Another amenity of Gwendolyn's is its convenient location near many historic, cultural, and natural sites. There are many downhill and cross-country skiing areas within a short drive while those with warm weather preferences can enjoy hiking, biking, golfing, and canoeing. The Weathersfield area features several state parks and nature areas for bird watching.

Laurie's determination to find a suitable career that would allow her to use her artistic talents and still be at home with her daughter, Gwendolyn, is what led the family to Vermont. The single-family mansion became Gwendolyn's Inn in 1990, and today, Laurie is fortunate enough to have the same opportunity while raising her 8-year old son, Michael.

Laurie enjoys collecting vintage clothing. She goes beyond displaying her collection, she wears it. She occasionally wears her vintage garb to serve afternoon tea, a highlight at Gwendolyn's. She serves hot or cold tea depending upon the season with an array of home-baked goodies or cheeses and fresh fruit.

RIGHT AND BELOW: INNKEEPER LAURIE HATHAWAY HAS A RATHER DIFFERENT APPROACH TO DISPLAYING HER COLLECTIBLES. LAURIE COLLECTS VINTAGE CLOTHING. SHE OFTEN WEARS HER VINTAGE CLOTHING DURING TEATIME FOR THE GUESTS. IN ADDITION, SHE HAS CLOTH MANNEQUINS THROUGHOUT THE INN ON WHICH SHE DISPLAYS CERTAIN COSTUMES.

The Great Valley House of Valley Forge

Valley Forge, Pennsylvania

Pattye Benson

Vintage Wedding Dresses

ABOVE: THE GREAT VALLEY HOUSE OF VALLEY FORGE DATES BACK TO 1690 AND IS ONE OF A FEW 17TH CENTURY STRUCTURES IN PRIVATE HANDS IN THIS COUNTRY.

The Great Valley House of Valley Forge dates back to 1690 and is one of the few 17th century structures in private ownership in this country. In 1681, Charles II granted a royal charter to William Penn for Pennsylvania. William Penn then granted land to John ap John, chief disciple of Quakerism in Wales. This subdivision was originally known as the Welsh Tract and covered what is now known as Main Line Philadelphia. There were many squatters and informal leases pertaining to this land from 1681 through the 1700s. The Great Valley House was built during this time as evident by the stone sink built into part of the stone wall in the Old Kitchen. This was typical of Welsh

construction prior to the use of a dry sink in 1690s. Thus, the Great Valley House is not only a wonderful bed and breakfast, but also an exceptional piece of living history.

In 1983, just one year after purchasing the home, Pattye decided to be one of the first bed and breakfasts in the Philadelphia area. After 19 years, she is surprised that she still enjoys the opportunity to share her home with visitors. During those 19 years, the inn has evolved in many ways, but it is still a preferred choice for honeymooning couples, visiting parents of local college students, travelers interested in history, and corporate guests looking for an alternative to the impersonal environment of hotels. Some corporate guests have stayed each Sunday through Thursday for over a year!

Pattye's wedding dress collection evolved over the last few years from her interest in antique textiles and quilts. As a quilter, Pattye has filled the Great Valley House with restored and newly created quilts. Her interest in vintage clothing, and in wedding dresses in particular, seemed to be a natural development from antique textiles. Although she has many pieces of

Victorian clothing, Pattye has found that wedding dresses are often the best preserved because they were typically stored in a hope chest after the bride's big day so that her daughter might wear it some day. In many cases, the dresses were handmade with careful attention to detail such as ribbon, lace, and beading. Pattye's collection of vintage dresses is displayed on antique dress forms throughout the Great Valley House. They often make for interesting conversation, and many guests leave determined to find their great-grandmother's wedding dress in the attic in order to display in their own homes.

RIGHT: THE VINTAGE WEDDING DRESSES AS WELL AS OTHER VINTAGE CLOTHING ARE DISPLAYED ON ANTIQUE DRESS FORMS THROUGHOUT THE INN.

INSET: THOUGH WEDDING DRESSES ARE HER FAVORITE, PATTYE ALSO HAS OTHER VINTAGE CLOTHING IN HER COLLECTION.

BELOW: ITEMS THAT COMPLEMENT PATTYE'S CLOTHING COLLECTION ARE PURSES, GLOVES, AND OTHER FASHIONABLE ACCESSORIES OF THE DAY.

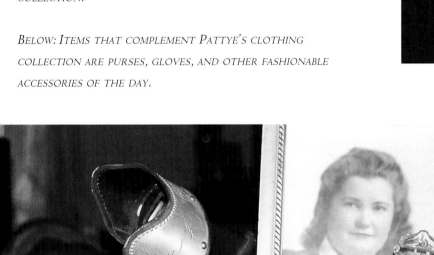

Colonel Taylor Inn

Cambridge, Ohio
James and Patricia Irvin

Quilts

ABOVE: THIS "PAINTED LADY" BOASTS 9,000 SQUARE FEET OF LIVING SPACE AND IS A STUNNING EXAMPLE OF VICTORIAN ARCHITECTURE.

INSET: PATRICIA USES HER QUILTS IN VARIOUS WAYS. SHE EVEN TAKES DAMAGED QUILTS APART TO MAKE THEM INTO THINGS SUCH AS THROW PILLOWS.

Built by Colonel Joseph D. Taylor, this beautiful three-story Victorian Mansion is the Colonel Taylor Inn. It has 9,000 square feet of living space and is located in the scenic part of southeastern Ohio. Colonel Joseph D. Taylor fought in the Civil War and served four terms as a United States Congressman. When he finished the house in 1878, it had 21 rooms and 11 fireplaces. The grand foyer welcomes guests with a regal carved staircase and oak hardwood floors. It is a striking example of Victorian architecture that captures all the charm and grace of a bygone era yet it has all the comforts and amenities expected of today's visitors.

Four spacious guestrooms are available on the second floor of the mansion each having its own fireplace, queen poster bed, and private bath. Guests may enjoy the formal dining room and parlor, curl up with a good book from the library, play a game or catch the game or a movie on the big screen television in the sitting room. Not only will visitors enjoy the history and grace of this "Painted Lady," but they also have the opportunity to explore the countryside. The Colonel Taylor is located near many state parks, craft shops, and antique malls. Visitors can hike, boat, fish, go horseback riding, ski or golf. Other nearby attractions include several glass factories and museums, the Living Word

Outdoor Drama, Georgetown Vineyards, the Zane Grey Museum, and the Longaberger Basket Company.

James and Patricia Irvin use their quilt collection in each of the four guestrooms. Guests can find them not only on their four-poster bed, but also thrown over chairs, used as table coverings, made into pillows and stacked high on antique chests.

RIGHT: HERE, PATRICIA CREATES A COLORFUL DISPLAY BY SIMPLY STACKING HER MANY QUILTS ON TOP OF AN ANTIQUE CHEST.

BELOW: QUILTS ARE USED IN DIFFERENT ASPECTS THROUGHOUT GUEST ROOMS WHETHER IT IS ON THE BED, TABLE, CHAIR, OR STACKED ON AN ANTIQUE CHEST.

INSET BELOW: ANOTHER UNCONVENTIONAL WAY THAT PATRICIA USES HER QUILTS IS BY DRAPING THEM OVER SIDE TABLES AS TABLECLOTHS. SHE USES A GLASS TOP ON THE TABLE FOR EASY CLEANING.

© Steve Taylor

Los Poblanos Inn
Albuquerque, New Mexico
Armin and Penny Rembe

Samplers and Beadwork

Listed on the New Mexico and the National Register of Historic Places, Los Poblanos Inn and La Quinta Cultural Center are located on 25 acres of agricultural fields and historic gardens. The Southwest's foremost architect, John Gaw Meem, who is known as the father of the Santa Fe style, designed both.

The Rembe family moved to Los Poblanos Ranch in 1977 and lived in the old ranch house. Armin's sister and her family lived in La Quinta, a 15,000 square foot house that was originally meant for entertaining and as an art center and library. After 25 years, Armin's sister decided to move to Ireland leaving the fate of the ranch up in the air. An architect friend of the Rembe family, Stefanos Polyzoides, convinced the Rembes to turn the house into an inn and return La Quinta to a Cultural

ABOVE: LOS POBLANOS INN IS JUST ONE PART OF THE ONGOING PROJECT TO RETURN LA QUINTA TO ITS ORIGINAL FUNCTION AS A CULTURAL CENTER.

INSET: THE INN'S MAGNIFICENT BLUE-TILED FOUNTAIN DECORATES THE COURTYARD.

Center as it was originally intended. This meant giving 14 acres to an agricultural trust so that it could never be developed as well as creating a very small cluster development on the farm.

Though there have been some stumbling blocks to this plan, Los Poblanos Inn is now up and running. Penny and Armin allowed a community supported organic agricultural project to tend to one of the fields in front of the property while they planted lavender in the other. They hold an annual lavender festival with the profits going to the Agricultural Committee of the Village of Los Ranchos.

Penny and Armin have several collections. One is an antique quilt collection that hangs in Armin's office. Armin is a hematologist and he felt that the quilts made the office a happy colorful place. He not only enjoys the quilts' beauty, but as he put it, "Only an optimist would begin a quilt," so it seemed appropriate to display such optimism throughout his office. Another collection that Penny and Armin own is one of Mexican samplers purchased at an estate sale. The samplers originally belonged to the daughter of the British Ambassador to Mexico. One of the samplers dates back to 1856.

ABOVE AND BELOW: THESE ARE TWO OF ARMIN AND PENNY REMBE'S MEXICAN SAMPLERS. THEY ORIGINALLY BELONGED TO THE DAUGHTER OF THE BRITISH AMBASSADOR TO MEXICO. ONE OF THE REMBE'S SAMPLERS DATES BACK TO 1856. THESE ARE FRAMED NOT ONLY FOR DECORATIVE PURPOSES, BUT TO PROTECT THEM.

Decorative and Holiday

Baskets
Shadow Boxes
Sheep
Smoking Paraphernalia
Snowbabies

The Pinnacle Vista Lodge

Little Rock, Arkansas

Chet and Linda Westergard

Snowbabies

Nestled on 28 wooded acres within the shadow of Pinnacle Mountain is Pinnacle Vista Lodge. This 6,000 square foot lodge has 3 cozy guestrooms and is framed by the scenic backdrop of nature's splendor found just outside the window of each room. It is the perfect escape from the rush of everyday life. Guests enjoy the challenging nature trails in the 2,000-acre Pinnacle Mountain State Park just a mile north of the lodge. A pile of car-sized boulders, Pinnacle Mountain rises 1,011 feet to overlook Little Rock and the surrounding area. For a less strenuous outing, throw a fishing line into the lodge's well-stocked pond or perhaps stay inside and play billiards on an antique Brunswick pool table. In addition, the state capital is just a short drive

ABOVE: THE PINNACLE VISTA LODGE IN ITS SPRING FINERY.

INSET: ONE OF THE MANY SNOWBABIES FIGURINES THAT CAN BE FOUND AT PINNACLE VISTA LODGE.

away and provides guests with plenty of opportunities for fine dining and shopping.

Snowbabies and antique/one-of-a-kind Santas are Linda's collectibles of choice. An experienced antique dealer, Linda's Snowbabies are grouped in scenes throughout the living areas of the lodge. The mantel, of course, is a perfect place to display a large scene of toddlers playing in the snow. Linda creates her scenes by covering a base of varying heights with quilt batting and then places her figurines in natural poses. She also uses the tops of old trunks and side tables as platforms for her scenes. Any flat surface can be transformed into a winter wonderland.

The origin of Snowbabies is unclear. There seems to be two major schools of thought on how the bisque figurines first came about. Many feel the popularity of Snowbabies began as early decorations for Christmas cakes. Traditional sweet cakes in Germany and Twelfth Night Cakes in England were commonly decorated with little creatures made of sugar as far back as the

96

beginning of the 19th century. By the late 1860s, the decorations led to the manufacture of more durable cake decorations made of porcelain that could be used year after year. These permanent decorations were made in Germany.

The other school of thought is based on the polar explorations of Admiral Peary and Dr. Cook. A fully-sculptured figurine of these two gentlemen dressed in Snowbaby suits and grasping a world globe between them further increases the credibility of this theory. In addition, a baby girl was born to the Peary family while in Greenland in 1893. The Eskimos called her Snow Baby because she was so white. Pairs of Snowbabies on sleds were made in celebration of the birth of the Peary's second child in 1910.

Between 1895 and 1905, Snowbabies with painted faces and dressed in white-hooded suits were made in Germany. Several companies manufactured them, but Hertwig & Company is generally credited to be the first to create the ones so familiar and prized by collectors today. Since 1986, Department 56 has introduced various collectible figurines. No matter how the first Snowbabies came about, there is a lasting appeal to these charming child-like figures hard at play in the snow.

BELOW: ANY FLAT SURFACE WILL DO, BUT OWNER LINDA WESTERGARD ENJOYS CREATING A LANDSCAPE OF WHITE ON HER FIREPLACE MANTEL TO SHOW OFF HER COLLECTION.

INSET: LINDA CREATES HER LANDSCAPE USING QUILT BATTING TO COVER THE VARYING HEIGHTS AND THE WHITE LIGHTS THAT BRING THE SCENE TO LIFE AT NIGHT.

Candlewyck Inn

Bigfork, Montana

Megan Vandergrift

Baskets

Open year round, Jorja Jane's Candlewyck Inn Bed and Breakfast is a majestic cedar and log home nestled among ten acres of handsome evergreens where one can often see Whitetail deer and wild turkey feeding. The inn offers two very spacious suites and six rooms with extremely comfortable beds accommodating the single guest as well as families or groups. Country folk art themes decorate each room. Guests enjoy a personalized country breakfast in the large dining area each morning.

The inn has massive front and back decks that encourage a certain appreciation for nature. Hiking and snowshoeing paths wind through the property for the outdoor types. Boating, golfing, hunting, and fishing are available throughout every season. Guests can even use

ABOVE: NESTLED AMONG TEN ACRES OF WOODLANDS, ONE CAN OFTEN SEE WHITETAIL DEER AND WILD TURKEY ON THE GROUNDS OF CANDLEWYCK INN.

the smoker grill provided for the fresh catch of the day. Or they can rent a boat, jet ski or take a wine and cheese sailboat cruise on Flathead Lake. For a more gentle outdoor activity, guests are invited to inner tube down Swan River for a relaxing afternoon. An ever-changing view can be found in every direction.

Those guests who are more interested in the inviting indoors have plenty to keep them occupied as well. Guests can take part in activities such as board games, puzzles, video movies for all ages, or a book from the owners' personal collection. In the evening, guests can gather for a cozy campfire.

The lodge style cedar and log home is the stage for many collections. These include a quilt collection many

ABOVE: HERE MEGAN VANDERGRIFT HANGS PIECES OF HER BASKET COLLECTION ALONG THE EXPOSED BEAMS OF THE SITTING ROOM. SHE ALSO HAS LARGE TRUNK-LIKE BASKETS BEHIND THE CHAIRS AND ALONG THE WALL FOR STORAGE.

of which are displayed on the wall hanging from special quilt clamps or from ordinary curtain rods. Others are found on beds or casually thrown over a chair. Santas are another collectible found during the holiday season at the inn. Vintage tin signs and colored glass bottles also adorn the lodge style home. Finally, the basket collection is both decorative and functional. Baskets of various styles and colors hang from the exposed beams while others are used as storage spaces for all sorts of everyday items that the innkeeper wants to hide from her guests' view.

Another Idea

Baskets are very versatile and can be both decorative and functional. Like boxes and trunks, baskets can be used for storage. This basket is actually a file cabinet.

The Wolcott House

Fenton, Michigan

Sean and Elaine Rosekrans

Smoking Paraphernalia

ABOVE: THE WOLCOTT HOUSE IS A FINE EXAMPLE OF
ITALIANATE ARCHITECTURE BUILT IN THE EARLY 1900S.

INSET: THIS ELEGANT PIPE IS JUST ONE OF THE MANY
EXAMPLES THAT SEAN ROSEKRANS OWNS. THIS ONE IS
DISPLAYED IN A VELVET BOX.

The Wolcott House is a stately red brick Italianate style home built near the turn of the century, and located in historic Fenton, Michigan. Once owned by the prominent Wolcott family, owners of the Wolcott Mill in downtown Fenton, the house is now a charming bed and breakfast establishment owned by Sean and Elaine Rosekrans. The home offers three beautiful guestrooms, each with its own unique decor. Full gourmet breakfast is served daily.

Built in the early 1900s, the Italianate style home eventually belonged to Anson (Ed) Wolcott and his wife, Lula May. Anson and Lula May Wolcott were married in 1904 and moved to the Fenton home in the early 1920s. This is the earliest family that the Rosekrans have been able to authenticate thus the inn's name. Mr. Wolcott, along with his brother Frank, owned and operated the historic Wolcott Mills. After his death in 1957, Anson Wolcott's family sold the home. It then became a retirement home for the ladies of the Christian Science Foundation and then for the Baptist Church who again sold it. Two other families owned the home before the Rosekrans purchased it in 1999. Vacant for over two years, the century old home needed extensive renovations.

Sean and Elaine came to own their bed and breakfast just a few short years ago. They opened for

ABVOE: THE ROSEKRANS' PARLOR IS DIVIDED IN THE SAME WAY AS THOSE OF THE 1900S—A LADY'S SIDE AND A GENTLEMAN'S SIDE. THE BUILT-IN CABINETS ON EITHER SIDE OF THE WINDOW EMPHASIZE THIS. THE BUILT-IN ON THE LEFT CONTAINS SEAN'S COLLECTION OF SMOKING PARAPHERNALIA.

INSET: HIS COLLECTION INCLUDES PIPES, TOBACCO TINS, AND HUMIDORS AMONG OTHER THINGS.

BELOW: THIS SIDE TABLE IS HOME TO SEVERAL PIPES DISPLAYED IN A PIPE HOLDER AS WELL AS LOOSELY ON THE TABLE ITSELF.

business in February 2001 after 18 months of renovations. They chose the Fenton area because it was near the center of Sean's sales territory where he represented a pharmaceutical company. The city of Fenton was delighted with the Rosekrans renovations, 99% of which they did themselves. The Wolcott House earned Sean and Elaine the Beautification Award for the city of Fenton in 2000.

Collecting for several years, Sean and Elaine have several collections displayed throughout their inn. They include over 200 giraffes, presidential memorabilia, cups and saucers, and Sean's collection of smoking paraphernalia. He currently has over 100 smoking related items including humidors, pipes, pipe racks, cuspidors, smoking stands, floor ashtrays, pictures, tin signs, lighters, cigar cutters, pipe tobacco making kits, and cigars. Most of Sean's display is located in the parlor, which is divided in much the same way as those during the 1900s—the lady's side and the gentleman's side.

The Whistling Swan Inn

Stanhope, New Jersey

Ron and Liz Armstrong

Longaberger Baskets

Nestled in a rural area of New Jersey, the house now known as the Whistling Swan Inn was built in 1905 by the justice of the peace, Daniel Best for his wife, Sarah. A founding family of Stanhope, the couple was in their sixties when they moved in and had an opening dinner party on November 11, 1905.

After passing through six families plus a mixture of abuse and "modernizations," this wonderful old house was restored to its turn-of-the century Victorian splendor and converted to a bed and breakfast in 1985. Eleven bathrooms have been added to the original house,

ABOVE: THE WHISTLING SWAN WELCOMES ANOTHER SUNNY MORNING.

INSET: HERE OWNER LIZ ARMSTRONG DISPLAYS SOME FAVORITE BEAR FRIENDS IN A LARGE LONGABERGER BASKET.

the ceilings have been returned to their original 10 feet, the wonderful tiger oak carved woodwork has been cleaned and polished, and the 10 bedrooms have been decorated in various antique themes.

The flavor of a vintage family home still permeates the Whistling Swan with everything from a friendly welcome and refreshments at arrival to a hearty breakfast on the pillared porch in the summer or by the fire in the dining room in the winter.

Guests are invited to relax on the porch overlooking the Victorian garden and swan fountain; read the morning paper in a porch rocker; swing on the porch swing; take a nap in the side-yard hammock; or sit in the inn's parlor or dining room with new-found friends.

Ron and Liz purchased the Whistling Swan Inn in the fall of 2000. The Armstrongs owned their own

LEFT: LONGABERGER BASKETS ARE
ESPECIALLY EASY TO USE BECAUSE
THE COMPANY HAS MADE SO
MANY SPECIALTY BASKETS SUCH
AS THE BUSINESS CARD HOLDER
SHOWN HERE.

BELOW: LIZ'S LONGABERGER
BASKET FILLED WITH FLOWERS
REFLECTS THE STENCILED VINE
AND FLOWERS ON THE TALL
FREESTANDING CABINET.

business during the 1980s and Liz yearned to be her own boss again. As an owner of a bed and breakfast, Liz could utilize her culinary skills from her previous job as operations manager of a food manufacturing plant as all as her love of decorating and Longaberger baskets. "You have to love people to stay at a bed and breakfast, and that is what brought us to own a bed and breakfast," explains Liz.

Longaberger baskets have long been a passion of Liz's. Introduced by her sister over 10 years ago, Liz has been collecting Longaberger baskets ever since. Liz feels that the beauty and longevity of the baskets make Longaberger a true American beauty. Having an inn makes a great showcase for the baskets because they are not only decorative, but they are useful as well. The baskets create a homey feeling and make the inn a unique place for guests to stay. Longaberger also makes pottery pieces that are used extensively at the inn. The serving pieces are used to serve breakfast dishes such as Apple Cranberry Casserole and the Longaberger coffee mugs are used on the hospitality bar for the guests' coffee and tea.

Alexander Hamilton House

Croton-on-Hudson, New York

Barbara Notarius

1920s Shadow Boxes

This stately Victorian Home located on a cliff above the river was Westchester's first bed and breakfast. The Alexander Hamilton House, circa 1889, is a short walk to the picturesque village of Croton-on-Hudson, gateway to New York's Hudson River Valley. It is close to Tarrytown, White Plains, Kykuit, Sunnyside, Lyndhurst, Boscobel, IBM and West Point, and is only one hour from New York City.

Alexander Hamilton House has four rooms and four suites. Five have fireplaces. The Bridal Chamber is the whole third floor of the inn with pink marble fireplace, king-sized bed, and breakfast served in the suite. No matter whether a guest stays out of business or pleasure, his or her stay at the Alexander Hamilton House will be a memorable one.

Unlike so many bed and breakfasts, Alexander Hamilton House has a 35-foot in-ground pool that is open Memorial Day to Labor Day. Other outdoor activities for guests include hiking, mountain biking, horseback riding, golf, and sailing on the Hudson. September through November is especially fun as it is apple picking season in the Hudson Valley. There are many fine orchards where guests can pick their own apples. For guests who prefer less strenuous activities, there are local wineries and several shopping areas nearby. West Point, Kykuit, the Rockefeller Estate and Art Center, and the Rockefeller archives are all nearby, as is the Storm King Art Center and Outdoor Sculpture Garden. The Croton Dam however, is still considered the local best kept secret.

ABOVE: THE PARLOR OF THE ALEXANDER HAMILTON HOUSE PLAYS CENTER STAGE TO MANY OF BARBARA'S SHADOW BOXES.

BELOW: FLOWERS WERE VERY SYMBOLIC AT THE TURN OF THE 20TH CENTURY—EACH HAD A SPECIFIC MEANING. THAT WAS ESPECIALLY IMPORTANT FOR A BRIDAL WREATH SUCH AS THIS.

Innkeeper, Barbara Notarius, is the successful owner of the Alexander Hamilton House and author of *Open Your Own Bed & Breakfast*. Barbara offers special three-day seminars, as well as a limited number of internships at her inn, while also being available for private consultation. She also owns Alexander Hamilton West in southern California.

ABOVE LEFT: THIS SHADOW BOX HAS A DISPLAY OF DRIED AND FAKE FLOWERS.

ABOVE RIGHT: THIS 1920S CREWELWORK IS FRAMED IN A COMPLEMENTARY GOLD FRAME.

Another Idea

You can use shadow boxes to display many different types of collectibles. Here, Sean and Elaine Rosekrans display some of their smoking paraphernalia such as pipes in a shadow box.

Pleasant Springs Farm

Boyd, Maryland

Jim and Peg Coleman

Sheep Figurines

ABOVE: *THOUGH IT IS ONLY 28 MILES FROM THE NATION'S CAPITOL, THIS RESTORED HAND-HEWN LOG CABIN IS UTTERLY SECLUDED FROM THE HUSTLE AND BUSTLE OF LIFE.*

INSET: *SOME OF PEG COLEMAN'S REAL LIFE COLLECTIBLES.*

Built circa 1768, the Drury/Austin House is on the National Register of Historic Places. It was built by Thomas Drury, an English settler to the colonies. The original house was constructed of hand-hewn chestnut beams. In 1840, Jonathan Austin purchased the tobacco farm and added the framed section of the home. The Austin family abandoned the cottage in 1951.

Though it is only 28 miles from Washington, D.C., the cottage is utterly secluded. Guests can sit on the front porch by candlelight, listen to the wildlife and watch the fireflies - the traffic and bustle are too far away to be heard. Downstairs is a log sitting room with fireplace, small kitchen, bedroom, and full bath with antique footed tub. Upstairs is a second log sitting room with sleep sofa, a double bedroom overlooking the garden, and a half bath.

Passionate about local history and with a degree in the subject, Peg Coleman researched and wrote a book, *Montgomery County: A Pictorial History*. At the same time, she began searching for an old house to purchase. Friends told them of the log cabin. The Colemans scrambled through thickets of greenbrier and poison ivy to find the forgotten home. As they approached, they could see that the doors and windows were gone. Then they stepped inside - fallen plaster, fireplace pulled apart, stairs missing, tree growing from the cellar, and a family of black vultures raising their family in the upstairs. The Colemans bought the neglected log cabin and spent the next 15 years restoring it. A bed and breakfast seemed to be the perfect use for such a log cabin and the Colemans found talented architects to assist with the restoration.

Already a sheep farmer, Peg increased her flock and her spinning. Of course, this was the perfect opportunity for friends to begin giving her sheep items, and the log cabin was a great place to display them. Now she buys sheep as well. Outside Peg decorates with the real thing!

Another Idea

When displaying collectibles, think about
other closely related items that you might use.
Here is a display of bluebirds. First, there are
different mediums – a figurine and a painting. Then
a bird's nest was added to complete the display.

*ABOVE: THE LOG CABIN HAS PROVIDED A WONDERFUL
BACKDROP FOR PEG'S SHEEP COLLECTION. THESE FEW ARE
DISPLAYED ALONG THE MANTEL OF THE BRICK FIREPLACE.*

*INSET: NOT ONLY DOES PEG DISPLAY HER SHEEP ON THE
MANTEL, SHE ALSO INCLUDES ITEMS THAT ARE CLOSELY
RELATED TO HER SHEEP SUCH AS SPINNING WHEELS AND A
WOMAN WITH HER WOOL YARN.*

Directory

55 East B &B - Art
55 East Street
Annapolis, MD 21401
Telephone: (410) 295-0202
Fax: (410) 295-0203
www.annearundelcounty.com/hotel/55east

Acacia House B & B - Saucers and Plates
158 Locust Ave.
Fairmont, WV 26554
Telephone: (304) 367-1000
Toll Free: (888) 269-9541
Fax: (304) 367-1000
www.acaciahousewv.com

Adventurers' Country B & B - Western and Indian Art
3803 I-80 S. Service Road
Cheyenne, WY 82009
Telephone: (307) 632-4087
Fax: (307) 632-4087
www.cruising-america.com/country.html

Alexander Hamilton House - 1920s Shadow Boxes
49 Van Wyck Street
Croton-on-Hudson, NY 10520
Telephone: (914) 271-6737
Fax: (914) 271-3927
www.alexanderhamiltonhouse.com

Arbor Rose B & B - Boxes
PO Box 114
Stockbridge, MA 01262
Telephone: (413) 298-4744
www.arborrose.com

Augusta House - Eastlake Furniture
49 South Street
Great Barrington, MA 01230
Telephone: (413) 528-3064
www.augustahouse.com

B & B at Taylor's Corner - Danish Porcelain
880 Route 171
Woodstock, CT 06281
Telephone: (860) 974-0490
Toll Free: (888) 503-9057
Fax: (860) 974-0498
www.bnbattaylorscorner.com

Bartlett House - Furniture
503 Front St
PO Box 159
Greenport, NY 11944
Telephone: (631)-477-0371
www.greenport.com/bartlett/welcome.htm

Bittersweet Farm - Crocks and Boxes
1720 St. Rt. 60
Millersburg, OH 44654
Telephone: (330) 276-1977

Black Forest B & B - Noah's Ark
11170 Black Forest Road
Colorado Springs, CO 80908
Telephone: (719) 495-4208
www.blackforestbb.com

Blue Heron Inn - Sports Memorabilia
P.O. Box 588
Findley Lake, NY 14736
Telephone: (716) 769-7852
Fax: (716) 769 7866
www.theblueheroninn.com

Brickhouse Inn - Pharmacy Bottles
452 Baltimore Street
Gettysburg, PA 17325
Telephone: (717) 338-9337
Toll Free: (800) 864-3464
Fax: (717) 338-9265
www.brickhouseinn.com

By the Side of the Road B & B -
Furniture
491 Garbers Church Road
Harrisonburg, VA 22801
Telephone: (540) 801-0430

Camden Windward - Plates
Six High Street
Camden, ME 04843
Telephone: 207-236-9656
Fax: 207-230-0433
www.windwardhouse.com

Cameo Rose Victorian Country Inn -
Dolls
1090 Severson Road
Belleville, WI 53508
Telephone: 608-424-6340
www.cameorose.com

Candlewyck Inn - Baskets
311 Aero Lane
Bigfork, MT 59911
Telephone: (406) 837-6406
Toll Free: (888) 617-8805
www.candlewyckeinn.com

Central Avenue House - Furniture
24 Central Avenue
Ocean Grove NJ 07756
Winter Telephone: (908) 598-1508
Summer Telephone: (732) 775-3579
www.centralavehouse.com

Charley Montana B & B - Fire King Dishes
PO Box 1192
Glendive, MT 59330
Toll Free: (888) 395- 3207
www.charley-montana.com

Chez Amis B & B - Teddy Bears
85 East Street
Annapolis, MD 21401
Telephone: 410-263-6631
Toll Free: 888-224-6455
Fax: 410-295-7889
www.chezamis.com

Colby Hill Inn - Teapots
PO Box 779
Henniker, NH 03242
Toll Free: (800) 531-0330
Telephone: (603) 428-3281
Fax: (603) 428-9218
www.colbyhillinn.com

Colonel Taylor Inn - Quilts
633 Upland Rd.
Cambridge, OH 43725
Telephone: (740) 432-7802
www.coltaylorinnbb.com

Corner George Inn B & B - Pitchers
Maeystown, Illinois
www.bbonline.com/il/cornergeorge/
room pictures/calendar of events/
registration form

Country Life B & B - Teddy Bears
67 Tabor Road
Greenwich, NY 12834
Telephone: (518) 692-7203
Toll Free: (888) 692-7203
Fax: (518) 692-9203
www.countrylifebb.com

Deerhill Inn - Yellow Ware
PO Box 136
West Dover, VT 05356
Telephone: (802) 464-3100
Toll Free: (800) 99 DEER 9
www.deerhill.com

Desert Dove B & B - Watt Pottery
11707 E. Old Spanish Trail
Tucson, AZ 85730
Telephone: (520) 722-6879
Toll Free: (877) 722-6879
www.desertdovebb.com

Dolls' House - Dolls
161 Green Street
Annapolis, MD. 21401
Telephone: (410) 626-2028
www.annapolis.net/dollshouse

Fitch Hill - Railroad Items
258 Fitch Hill Road
Hyde Park, VT 05655
Telephone: (802) 888-3834
Toll Free: (800) 639-2903
www.fitchhillinn.com

Gillum House - Dolls
35 Walnut Street
Shinnston, WV26431
Telephone: (304) 592-0177
Toll Free: (888) 592-0177
www.bbonline.com/wv/gillum

Golden Pheasant - Quimper
763 River Road (Route 32)
Erwinna, PA 18920
Telephone: (610) 294-9595
Toll Free: (800) 830-4474
Fax: (610) 294-9882
www.goldenpheasant.com

Governor's Trace - Dolls and Antique Toys
303 Capitol Landing Road
Williamsburg, VA 23185-4314
Toll Free: (800) 303-7552
Telephone : (757) 229-7552
Fax: (757) 220-2767
www.governorstrace.com

Gracehill - Purses
1169 Little Round Top Way
Townsend, TN 37882
Telephone: (865) 448-3070/3071
Fax: (865) 448-3077
www.gracehillbandb.com

Great Valley House of Valley Forge - Vintage Wedding Dresses
1475 Swedesford Road
Malvern, PA 19355
Telephone: (610) 644-6759
www.greatvalleyhouse.com

Gwendolyn's Inn - Vintage Clothes
Main Street
Perkinsville, VT 05151
Telephone: (802) 263-5248
Toll Free: (877) 493-6365
www.gwendolyns.com

Hodgdon Island Inn - Original Art
Barters Island Road
Box 492
Boothbay, ME 04571
Telephone: (207) 633-7474
www.hodgdonislandinn.com/#here2

Hutton House - Depression Glass and McCoy Pottery
Routes 250 and 219
PO Box 88
Huttonsville, WV 26273
Telephone: (304) 335-6701
Toll Free: (800) 234-6701
www.wvonline.com/shareourbeds/hutton

Inn at Norwood - Teapots
7514 Norwood Ave.
Sykesville, MD 21784
Telephone: (410) 549-7868
www.innatnorwood.com

Inn at Stockbridge - Pewter
PO Box 618 Rt 7 N
Stockbridge, MA 01262
Telephone: (413) 298-3337
Fax: (413) 298-3406
www.stockbridgeinn.com

Ivy Rose Cottage - Flow Blue China and White Ironstone
210 South Cearlock
Cheyenne, OK 73628
Telephone: (580) 497-3505
Toll Free: (877) 456-0403
www.ivyrose.net

Lewis House - Bayer Figurines
38 East High Street
Ballston Spa, NY 12020
Telephone: (518) 884-9857
www.lewishouse.com

Los Poblanos - Samplers
4803 Rio Grande Boulevard NW
Albuquerque, NM
Telephone: (505) 344-9297
Toll Free: (866) 344-9297
www.lospoblanos.com

Lynn's Inn B & B - Rare Books
614 W. Santa Fe Ave.
Flagstaff, AZ 86001
Telephone: (520) 226-1448
Toll Free: (800) 530-9947
www.lynnsinn.com

McKibbon House B & B Inn - Dept. 56
611 East Boundary Street
Montevallo, AL
Telephone: (205) 665-1275
www.mckibbonhouse.com

Mill Creek Homestead B&B - Dolls
2578 Old Philadelphia Pike
Bird-in-Hand, PA 17505
Telephone: (717) 291-6419
Toll Free: (800) 771-2578
Fax: (717) 291-2171
www.bbonline.com/pa/millcreek

Mill House Inn - Western and Indian Art
31 North Main Street
Long Island, NY 11937
Telephone: (631) 324-9766
Fax: (631) 324-9793
www.millhouseinn.com

Mr. Underfoot's Inn - Typewriters
9 North Main Street
Prattsburgh, NY 14873
Telephone: (607) 522-4754
www.bbonline.com/ny/mrunderfoot

Natchez Trace B & B - Vintage Photos
P. O. Box 193
Hampshire, TN 38461
Toll Free: (800) 377-2770
www.bbonline.com/natcheztrace

Notchland Inn - Cobalt Glassware
Route 302
Hart's Location, NH 03812
Toll Free: (800) 866-6131
www.notchland.com

Old Brick Inn - Vintage Tablecloths
PO Box 987
St. Michaels, MD 21663
Telephone: (410) 745-3323
Fax: (410) 745-3320
www.oldbrickinn.com

Oyster Point Inn - Art Nouveau Posters
www.oysterpointinn.com.

Parsonage on the Green - Teapots
20 Park Place
Lee, MA 01238
Telephone: (413) 243-4364
www.bbhost.com/parsonageonthegreeen

Pineapple Hill - Pineapples
1324 River Road
New Hope, PA 18938
Telephone: (215) 862-1790
Toll Free: (888) 866-8404
www.pineapplehill.com

Pinnacle Vista Lodge - Snowbabies
7510 Hwy 300
Little Rock, AR 72223
Telephone: (501) 868-8905
www.pinnaclevista.com

Pleasant Springs Farm - Sheep
16112 Barnesville Road
Boyd, MD 20841

President's Quarters Inn and
Guesthouse - Presidential Memorabilia
225 East President Street
Savannah, Georgia 31401
Telephone: (912) 233-1600
Toll Free: (888) 592-1812
Fax: (912) 238-0849
www.presidentsquarters.com

Queen Victoria® - Arts and Crafts
Furniture
102 Ocean Street
Cape May, NJ 08204
Telephone: (609) 884-8702
www.queenvictoria.com

Red Barn B&B - Quilts
733 Herricks Lane
PO Box 1602
Jamesport, NY 11947
Telephone: (631) 722-3695
www.northfork.com/redbarn/

Rosewood Country Inn - Teddy Bears
Pleasant View Road
Bradford, NH 03221
Telephone: (603) 938-5253
Toll Free: (800) 938-5273
www.bbonline.com/nh/rosewood

Stone Soup Inn - China
1304 North Central Avenue
Indianapolis, IN 46202
Telephone: (317) 639-9550
Fax: (317) 684-9536
www.stonesoupinn.com

State House Inn - Folk Art Animal
Collection
25 State Circle
Annapolis, MD 21401
Telephone: (410) 990-0024
Fax: (410) 990-9508
www.statehouseinn.com

Villa - Napkin Rings
705 N. 5th Street
Tacoma, WA 98403
Telephone: (253) 572-1157
Toll Free: (888) 572-1157
Fax: (253) 572-1805
www.villabb.com

Waterloo Country Inn - Clocks &
Coffee Grinders
28822 Mt. Vernon Road
Princess Anne, MD 21853
Telephone: (410) 651-0883
Fax: (410) 651-5592
www.waterloocountryinn.com

Wedgwood Inn - Wedgwood
33 Old Mill Road
New Hope, PA 18938
Telephone: (215) 862-2570
www.new-hope-inn.com

Whispering Pines - Pottery
60 Cedar Hill Road
High Falls, NY 12440
Telephone: (845) 687-2419
www.whisperingpinesbb.com

Whistling Swan - Longaberger Baskets
110 Main Street
Stanhope, NJ 07874

Wolcott House - Smoking Paraphernalia
610 W. Silver Lake Road
Fenton, MI 48430
Telephone: (810) 714-4317
Fax: (810) 714-4318
www.thewolcotthouse.com